THE
"RIPE"
TIME

THE
"RIPE"
TIME

DR. GWENDOLYN GAUT
XULON PRESS

Xulon Press
2301 Lucien Way #415
Maitland, FL 32751
407.339.4217
www.xulonpress.com

Unless otherwise indicated, Scripture quotations taken from the King James Version (KJV)–*public domain.*

Scripture quotations taken from the New King James Version (NKJV). Copyright © 1982 by Thomas Nelson, Inc. Used by permission. All rights reserved.

Scripture quotations taken from the Holy Bible, New International Version (NIV). Copyright © 1973, 1978, 1984, 2011 by Biblica, Inc.™. Used by permission. All rights reserved.

Scripture quotations taken from the Amplified Bible (AMP). Copyright © 1954, 1958, 1962, 1964, 1965, 1987 by The Lockman Foundation. Used by permission. All rights reserved.

Paperback ISBN-13: 978-1-6628-2034-2

Ebook ISBN-13: 978-1-6628-2035-9

DEDICATION

As I wrote this book, many along this journey inspired and pushed me to write and share God's revelation.

I dedicate this book to those who encouraged me to never give up and stay the course. Donna Avery, who saw the vision and reminded me of the importance of others needing to read the revelation during these times in the World. She also was my eyes in pre-editing the book.

My brother Anthony who helped me format the manuscript and was my technical support while putting the chapters in place.

Both started this journey with me, but God now has them as they Rest in Peace.

My God mother (Barbara) who always encouraged me to step out on FAITH and has been and continues to be the voice of reason and my listening ear.

Apostle Denise who has been my sister, confidant and Apostle who has and continues to pray for me and encouraged me to write as the HOLY SPIRIT would lead me, guide me, and instruct me too.

Reverend Dennis, my brother who saw in me, what I did not see in myself and encouraged me to go forth as GOD has ordained. Also praying for me and wanting the best for me.

My parents Sarah and Clarence who laid the foundation and never wavered in believing in me. They now are the Angels underneath my wings.

For those who I didn't mention you know who you are, and in any way you contributed to my journey I am grateful.

I thank you all for being a part of the journey, and I hope to make you all proud.

TABLE OF CONTENTS

FOREWORD

We all have a ripe or right time to start our journey. In this book the author uses metaphors, acronyms, analogies, anagrams, and the like to present a familiar ring to the Biblical verses. The use of Jehovah, God, and Jesus respects all religions, and the author invites the reader to use discipline as they embark on a journey that encourages us to think deeply about our changes, improvement, challenges, and other forces that will help our journey.

If we must interrupt our busy lives, to sit and listen, and to reflect or adjust our lives in the search for peace we should take the time to do it.

This collection of Biblical readings and the above examples of the grammatical syntax allows us to take both a serious and whimsical journey so that we choose the right paths that make us ripe enough to pick from the tree of life in our search for peace. Finally, I like the fact that the author has even left room for you to make notes as you travel on this journey.

Louisia Fuller AKA Professor Donna L. Avery

Now Is The Ripe Time

To follow God and see where the journey takes you.
To follow the Master Leader, so you can become one of
His leaders.
To follow His instructions to find possibilities that are endless.
Once your fruit is ripened, Jehovah will pick you for His work
and purpose

CHAPTER ONE

"A COMMON THREAD"

Psalm 139:13-15
For You formed my inward parts; You covered me in my moth-
er's womb. I will praise You, for I am fearfully and wonderfully
made; Marvelous are Your works, And that my soul knows very
well. My frame was not hidden from You, When I was made in
secret, And skillfully wrought in the lowest parts of the earth.

A common thread is an idiom used to refer to a recur-
ring or similar characteristic present in different
situations or circumstances. For example, when a
detective is studying a crime, he looks for similarities
to previous crimes. This helps him to understand the criminal
and track him down. These similarities are a common thread
that tie the criminal to his crime. Similarly, a common
thread we all must consider is allowing God to thread His
needle and start "sewing" the pieces of our lives together.

It is important to note that sewing is an ongoing
process. When God is "sewing" our garment it might
require some additions, deletions, edits, and
rewrites to the pieces of our journey as we hear

from God. Always try to follow the leader and the instructions closely. It may take days, months, or even years of listening, writing, and learning during our quiet time with Him.

Remember, just like any journey, there are many steps to the process. The garment you are "sewing" is a work in progress, so let God help you through the process. You must let Him carefully choose the textile fiber and smoothly cut the material or cloth with the correct scissors. As He "sews," He must make sure the thread color matches perfectly and that the thread travels through the correct size of needle. I know right away you are thinking, *This sounds hard. I need a sewing machine!* Nope, you do not. To prepare your patience for this journey, think of slowly HAND SEWING this garment. That way, you are constantly reminded and know this will take time.

To protect yourself, avoid any guilt and do not try to finish your garment quickly. Move forward slowly, as you proceed, so the fit is correct when you finish your garment

REFLECTIONS AND NOTES:

1. What is something that you are currently working on in your life that you are sewing and need help from Jehovah to complete?

2. Or possibly you are stuck and do not know what the next step should be in the sewing process.

3. Take note of where you are in the process and retrace your steps and review each stitch you sewed into the process. You may have to undo some of your work on your garment but is not it better to undo a piece of the work than an entire garment.

ROOM TO JOURNAL

_____

_____

_____

_____

_____

_____

_____

_____

_____

_____

_____

_____

_____

_____

CHAPTER TWO

"LIFE'S CAR RIDE"

Judges 18: 5-6 "Then they said to him, 'Please inquire of God to learn whether our journey will be successful,' The priest answered them, 'Go in peace Your journey has the Lord's approval.'"

We often compare life to a journey. In this chapter, we will explore the peace we can find by allowing God to be our driver on life's journey.

As I continue to write this book, I explore another metaphorical experience where I take life's journey, finding peace while allowing God to take the wheel of my car.

This journey of life, seen as a car ride, is completed with the complete assistance of God. It could be His Son, Jesus, giving us specific instructions and navigating us through the difficult detours in our life; the Holy Spirit leading and guiding us to our destination; or everything combined together.

It becomes important to not try getting into the driver's seat with God, or the passenger seat with Jesus. Take your seat in the back and enjoy the scenery of the beautiful world God has made. Allow the Holy Spirit to work inside you.

We all know, when we get in a car for a long journey, we will make a few pits stops to get gas, something to eat, or go to the bathroom. When making these necessary stops, we must be diligent not to be distracted. Perhaps the person serving us food asks a few questions, *Where are you going?* or *Who is with you? Why are you traveling this road?* Maybe they interject with opinions or thoughts. *There is a quicker way to go.* Remember who is driving the car; it is easy to get blindsided by jibber-jabber that we allow to enter our ears' gate. Let Jehovah be your chauffer. Guard your ears and heart to only hear from God. Allow Jesus to give you directions to follow and the Holy Spirit to lead us by a map that is an exclusive blueprint designed just for your journey. They all work together as one.

MAINTAINING YOUR CAR

Continuing our metaphor of a car trip, we need to properly prepare. We already have the best driver, navigator, and best guide; now we need one more thing. Maintenance for our car.

Cars require constant maintenance. An overall tune-up, oil change, brake or brake pad replacement, top off power steering fluid, engine check, new battery, oil change, heating or air conditioning repairs – the list seems to never end. Before we continue on a trip, we must attend to these numerous and important repairs. Only then, may we continue with our journey.

Let us start with an overall tune-up. An overall tune-up is a basic preventive maintenance performed on a vehicle to ensure it continues to perform. The mechanic checks all the interacting parts for wear to ensure that the vehicle maintains its highest performance. Finding the right mechanic to service the car is crucial. We should choose someone with experience working on our type of vehicle. To be safe, we choose one of the angels. With an angel as our mechanic, assigned by Jehovah, we can trust any repairs or tune-up our car will experience.

When a mechanic works on a car, he/she must open the hood and do a diagnostic test. This diagnostic will show the mechanic what needs to be repaired on the car. Similarly, Jehovah may run a "diagnostic test" to see where we need maintenance in our life. We must be prepared for repairs in one or all issues the diagnostic reveals.

LIST OF REPAIRS

Oil Change: Changing the oil is when the OLD engine oil is removed and replaced with FRESH engine oil so that the engine oil does not breakdown or wear out too soon. If we want to compare our journey to a car ride, changing the oil lubricates the engine, absorbs any heat, and allows for high efficiency. Changing the oil, taking the OLD oil out and replacing with new oil, or a fresh anointing, and a tune-up where all the parts are checked to ensure everything will work in tandem and perform well. Your heart, mind, body, and soul are working on one accord.

Brakes: Maintain the brakes and brake pads. They apply pressure to the wheels and allows the rotors to stop the car. Brake rotors are also called discs, they allow the brake pads to clamp down and stop the wheels from spinning. Your brakes and brake pads are critical to ensuring you can stop when Jehovah gives the order.

Power Steering: Next is the steering wheel fluid, the power steering fluid is the hydraulic fluid that transmits the power into the steering system. Power steering allows the pressure to easily steer the car in the direction your map is taking you. The steering wheel can move you in the direction you are being led by Jehovah.

Engine: The engine is a machine which allows the car to have movement. It is designed to use energy, especially heat energy. The combustion (energy) that occurs causes the engine, and thus the car, to move. The Holy Spirit—the engine—which is the main component of the car, starts and supplies power to the vehicle.

Battery: The battery of a car is a chargeable device that supplies electrical current to a motor vehicle. Its main purpose is to feed the starter, which will start the engine. Keep the battery in good condition. It charges the vehicle and sends electricity to all parts of the car to function. Every time you pray, or fast, listen to the silence so you can hear His voice, read the Word. In this, even when you are kind and helping others, you are recharging yourself and others.

Temperature Control: Allow Jehovah to regulate the temperature inside and outside the car. This way, your mind and body can adjust to whatever situations or circumstances will equip you to continue your journey. If the weather in your life or journey calls on you to check your heating, ventilation, and air condition system – better known as the HVAC – it is allowing you to adjust the climate around you. With HVAC working properly, you can be comfortable by keeping filters, electronic sensors, and all other moving parts clean.

As you can see, even when we follow instructions to a tee, we do not always know where Jehovah is taking us but stay tuned to Him. Your directions will become crystal clear as we prepare the car for the journey.

ROOM TO JOURNAL

_____

_____

_____

_____

_____

_____

_____

_____

_____

_____

_____

_____

_____

_____

_____

CHAPTER THREE

"SHINE SO BRIGHT"

Psalm 27:1 "The Lord is my light and my salvation whom shall I fear? The Lord is the strength of my life; of whom shall I be afraid?"

My daughter and son, I am your light. I want you to shine brightly. Wherever you go, I will be with you. Anytime you start feeling afraid or fear creeps up in your spirit, recite this scripture above or this below given to me in my quite time with Jehovah.

I, Jehovah, will bring peace and rest to your spirit. Burn the fear and being afraid as I am with you always even to the end. Amen.

I am refining you in that fire. It is a process. While you go through it, be anxious for nothing. Remember, I am working it out for your good and my Glory. Seek peace like a river, which flows quietly in your soul.

CONSIDER THIS ANALOGY:

When you buffer a wood floor, you take it down to the original wood. You take out all the scuffmarks, the dirt, the accumulated wax and anything else that has built up. During this stripping, the wood is being prepared for a new coat of wood polish that allows the wood to shine. The same is true in our lives. Jehovah strips us of experiences, thoughts or beliefs that "dirty" us. When he is finished, we are ready to be polished by His Holy Spirit. You'll be so polished that you may almost see the reflection of Jehovah in everything you do.

SIT AND LISTEN:

Jehovah is doing a new thing in you. He is watching, He is there; there is no reason to fear. Concentrate on you. Sit and/or listen as the new wood is being polished.

REFLECTIONS AND NOTES:

Ask yourself what decisions or actions in your life are dulling your shine or causing scuffmarks on your floor?

ROOM TO JOURNAL

_____

_____

_____

_____

_____

_____

_____

_____

_____

_____

_____

_____

_____

_____

CHAPTER FOUR

"NEVER LOOK BACK"

Psalm 9:1 "I will praise You O Lord, with my whole heart; I will tell of Your marvelous works."

T he Psalms speak of your enemies being turned back and you being protected through the process. It speaks of enemies being cut down where they will rise no more. It is important to note that God will do this, not us. Our job is to worship God with our whole heart, and He will perform the "marvelous works."

Along your journey, people will hurt you. They will speak against you, they may even do evil things to you, but you must not fret. You must not look back on these problems as you continue forward in your life. You must pray for people who do these things and forgive them. As Jesus said on the cross,

"Father, forgive them, for they know not what they do."

CONSIDER THIS ANALOGY:

When a person crosses the street, the premise is they are trying to get to the other side safely. As they step off the curb, they must focus on the traffic in front of them. Not behind. Looking back at the curb they've left will normally cause danger.

Compare this to life. We cannot look backward because distractions will cause problems. Focusing on your past can cause us to become stuck in a negative situation or way of thinking. It may cause us to be afraid of crossing the street. We cannot be afraid to look forward and cross. Staying at one point will not rid us of past negative experiences. As we cross the road to cleanse our hearts, we must also forgive ourselves and/or others. We must be honest with ourselves and if we are the ones at fault, we must repent. Then, as we hear or see the word WALK, we need to cross right away. Once you get to the other side, you can walk into your present and prepare for the next crossing in your future. Know that each crossing will bring new challenges. Let the Holy Spirit instruct you as you move forward.

Nothing is easy as one, two, three, but be encouraged and courageous. Anytime you feel any discomfort, squeeze His hand and let Him squeeze back. Transfer your fears to the Master Teacher. Follow Jehovah's Lead. Take His hand and never let go.

REFLECTIONS AND NOTES

1. What are you afraid to walk into, or walk away from?

2. Do not let the fear of the unknown stop you from your future.

3. The challenge is to step out, but do not look back only move forward.

ROOM TO JOURNAL

_____

_____

_____

_____

_____

_____

_____

_____

_____

_____

_____

_____

_____

CHAPTER FIVE

"PERFORMANCE OF A LIFETIME"

Psalm 99:3. Let them praise your great and awesome name-
He is Holy.

Psalm100:1-2, Make a joyful shout to the Lord, all you
lands! Serve the Lord with gladness; Come before His presence
with singing.

W hen you hear this term "performance of a lifetime," many things may come to mind. Maybe an incredible role in a play, an amazing game in a sport, or a perfect singing performance at a concert. In the context of these Psalms, we stand before God in His Holy presence and worship him with our lives.

The definition of "performance" is an act of staging or presenting a play, concert, or other form of entertainment. Also defined as the action or process of carrying out or accomplishing an action, task, or function.

The definition of "lifetime" is the duration of a thing's existence or usefulness.

As you prepare for this performance of a lifetime, it is important to read God's word, rehearse and learn your lines. Know your audience, study to show yourself improved, pray that you will make a difference in someone's life. Listen to the director Jehovah as He prepares you for the performance. Then once the lights and stage are prepared, step out and give the 'performance of a lifetime". Our entire life performance should be reflective of worshipping God in song and praise daily, entering into his courts with thanksgiving and praise.

CONSIDER THIS ANALOGY:

Imagine that you are an actor and you have just performed in a play. The performance is over and the audience is applauding as the actors gather for the final curtain call. The star of the show walks out and the applause crescendos to a deafening roar. You may be disappointed that the audience did not give you such a thunderous applause for your performance. Don't be discouraged. As long as you did exactly what the director (Jehovah) told you to, you have done a wonderful job. Take your bow with your head held high and when the director comes out, turn all attention to him. When you take your final bow at this Final Curtain Call, the curtain is lowered for the last time and it is time to start a new day.

When we pray, we clasp our hands, close our eyes, get on our knees, seek a quiet place, or perform as we bow to Jehovah. When we pray, "without ceasing," so to speak, we may do any combination of these performances. Will you be ready? Just like a stage performance worshipping, exalting, praising, serving, and other forms of recognizing Jehovah are best done in our hearts. Perform for the Master Director, not for others. In every scene, make sure you perform as directed. Stay ready for the next scene. Again, the recognition received is not important. It is important to follow the script Jehovah gave to *you*.

Ironically, as the performer, you might not acknowledge that bowing is a gesture, which shows humility and deep respect for someone. Do you have deep respect for God or Jehovah?

SIT AND LISTEN:

Bow before God, worship him in spirit and in truth. In his presence, we bow to honor Him. Bow to show your respect. Be reminded that we must perform and act as He instructs us to. Always know that although we may benefit our brothers and sisters through our actions, we are performing for God, not for man.

Have we given our best performance for God?

REFLECTIONS AND NOTES

1. What performance are you currently preparing for in life?

2. Have you studied your lines given and ready to go on stage and follow the director's instructions?

ROOM TO JOURNAL

_____

_____

_____

_____

_____

_____

_____

_____

_____

_____

_____

_____

_____

CHAPTER SIX

"OUR VICTORY IS IN GOD"

BE ANXIOUS FOR NOTHING

Psalm 10: 1-4, 12, 14 -Why do You stand afar off, O Lord? Why do You hide in times of trouble? The wicked in his pride persecutes the poor; Let them be caught in the plots which they have devised. For the wicked boasts of his heart's desire; He blesses the greedy and renounces the Lord. The wicked in his proud countenance does not seek God; God is in none of his thoughts.

Arise, O Lord! O God, lift up Your hand! Do not forget the humble. But you have seen, for You observe trouble and grief, To repay it by Your hand. The helpless commits himself to You; You are the helper of the fatherless.

P salm 10 is "A Song of Confidence in God's Triumph over Evil." It references the wickedness of man. It relates to us how man thinks he can continue to mistreat those who are less fortunate and satisfy his greed for fulfilling his desires at any cost.

The pandemic of 2020 as we knew as the coronavirus, COVID-19 during this time brought out the many injustices and inequalities as man became more divided in addressing the needs of those who were affected by the virus directly or indirectly. We live in a world promoting defiance, wickedness, evil, greed, and all the things the world is facing. Leaders are being challenged, the rich are pacifying the underserved with huge donations, people are addressing the plight of the underserved in all areas like never.

Unfortunately, through all this, the backdrop is consistent, "the good suffer with the bad." We may be tempted to ask the question. Who is good and who is bad? Who should suffer?

Since none of us can pass judgment, all of us are challenged to neither waver, fear, nor despair during this time. That is a challenge, but since God sees everything and knows everything, we may not understand why these things are occurring. We should always do what is best for others while we stay solid in our faith. We must trust the processes, the changes, and all that is taking place while we know that He is King of kings and the Lord of lords.

As we read Philippians 4, we learn the chapter speaks to us of gentleness, peace, honesty, and overall rejoicing, and especially in verses 5,7, and 8—God speaks to us.

In verse seven, He asks us to guard our hearts and minds. In verse eight, He asks us to meditate or think on these things.

After reflecting on the above words, I invite you to add words to what you see or hear in what you have read. Do not allow any distractions to enter as you meditate on these words.

CONSIDER THIS ANALOGY:

Think of the speed of a modern microwave and how it quickly heats up leftovers. The microwave is also fast when cooking a meal.

The magnetron unit in the microwave sends out waves, which emit heat from the center outward. It heats up fast. It defrosts frozen food. They are a popular item and have experienced incredible growth in sales because everyone wants to enjoy their food as quickly as possible.

Think of what is called a *conventional* oven. It is mostly used when we expect to preheat and cook slowly at a recommended temperature.

We must take the time to read the instructions when we prepare a dish in order to make sure the food is prepared properly.

The challenges we face are more like a conventional oven. These days food is packaged where the instructions give us a choice of which oven we will physically operate.

Ask yourself if the instructions from God will be operated slowly. If you know that your patience will be tried, and things will not manifest until he is ready, we will understand why I say our challenges will best materialize in the conventional oven.

Think about it, we want things quickly, but that is usually not our reality. So many times, we go through trial and error before even beginning to follow the instructions.

However, if we take the time to read the instruction manual, which in this case is listening to God's Word, we can save ourselves a lot of hardships by not rushing through the process.

REFLECTION AND NOTES:

1. Have you ever skipped a step or process due to impatience? What kind of problems did it cause?

2. Was rushing and skipping the process worth it in the end? Did it help you achieve your desired outcome?

ROOM TO JOURNAL

CHAPTER SEVEN

"FOLLOW THE LEADER

Matthew 10 (The Twelve Apostles) challenges us to wonder if we can follow or lead as the Twelve Disciples did.

When Jesus sent his disciples to minister around the world, He gave them certain responsibility and specific instructions. They were given the power and responsibility to cast out unclean spirits and heal all kinds of sickness and disease. As they were sent out, they were told not to go by the way of the Gentiles. Jesus told them not to go the city of Samaria, not to preach to the lost sheep of Israel. He told them to know that the Kingdom of God was at hand, to greet everyone they meet on the path, to travel of the beaten path. He told them to pray for others without judgment of who the person was or what they had done.

He also gave a very practical instruction. If they preached or prayed somewhere and the message was accepted, they were to thank the person and leave in peace. But if someone rejected their prayer or message, they were to wipe the dust off their feet and keep moving. We should have the same approach to life. God has a mission for all of use. Our job is to take the time to listen and understand what he wants us to do. Some may be called to one city and others may not. We must know and follow what God has for us.

It is also important to understand that our job is to follow God's instructions, not the results of doing so. We, of course, are excited when our message or prayer is received and we should celebrate. However, not everyone will receive the word. You will be persecuted for sharing the message of Jehovah. Some will try to get you in legal trouble, others will leave negative messages on social media or report you to those in authority. When people refuse to hear or listen to what message you bring, shake the dust of your feet and leave. In other words, don't let that situation distract or disappoint you. Shake it off and keep moving. The disciples followed Jesus because they believed in Him and trusted Him. Also, He had proven He was a man of His word and had a track record of being a doer and not just a hearer of the Word. He lived it out daily. Keeping your word and getting people to trust the God in you is the first step in displaying the leadership qualities of a person of integrity.

Do not let these people and persecutors steal your joy or peace in following God. Rather, find your bravery and stand your ground. Look to the Word of God for your inspiration. Look to those we now consider heroes and draw strength from this instruction: Do not worry because when it is time to speak, and Jehovah has given you what to say and how to say it, so you can be brave in your heart. Let Jesus be your teacher and instructor.

CONSIDER THIS ANALOGY:

We have all heard the phrase follow the leader. When we follow someone or their instructions we usually do so because we agree with what they are doing or saying, and they have a good track record.

So now, reflect a minute. Are you a leader or a follower? Given different circumstances, there is nothing wrong with being both as the circumstances dictate. The disciples often did this, and you can too. However, as Matthew 10 unfolds, Jesus prepares them to be leaders. So, we must all be followers at some point so we can then learn how to lead.

Where are you in this process? Can you be a good follower? Take instructions that give you a strong foundation for becoming a leader. Never dismiss a follower. Most of the people in the Bible were followers and learned how to become great leaders.

Moses had been discovered as a child, he was plucked from the river then raised as an Egyptian. Moses was a part of God's plan. He was prepared to assume the role of a leader and lead his people out of bondage. He followed the instructions of Jehovah and became a great leader because he followed instructions.

Do not ever underestimate a follower, because tomorrow that person can become the leader.

Learn and be respectful when you are in either role, so you know what is required when you are asked to step into either one. Both roles are important to Jehovah. He can investigate our hearts to see if we are ready for either role.

SIT AND LISTEN
Study the following anagram

L - listen	F - fighter
E - equality	O - ownership
A - assertive	L - loyal
D - diligent	L - listening
E - eager	O - overcome unpleasant
R - responsible	circumstances
	W - willingness to accept
	a challenge
	E - enlightenment
	R - respectful

You may see other words here. Write them down as you think of either leading or following. All the leaders and followers need each other. How do you see them? Where do you see yourself?

ROOM TO JOURNAL

CHAPTER EIGHT

"COMMANDMENTS TO LIVE BY"

TEN COMMANDMENTS

*Deuteronomy 10: 1-5 At that time the Lord said to me.
Hew for yourself two tablets of stone like the first and come
up to Me on the mountain and make yourself an ark of wood.
And I will write on the tablets the words that were on the first
tablets, which you broke; and you shall put them in the ark. "
So I made an ark of acacia wood, hewed two tablets of stone
like the first, and went up the mountain, having the
two tablets in my hand. And He wrote on the tablets
according to the first writing, the Ten Commandments,
which the Lord had spoken to you in the mountain from the
midst of the fire in the day of the assembly; and the Lord gave
them to me. Then I turned and came down from the mountain, and put the tablets in the ark which I had made; and
there they are, just as the Lord commanded me,"*

Deuteronomy 10 speaks of God's instructions to
Moses to carve the second set of the Ten
Commandments tablets. The second set was

necessary because the people had become corrupted into idolatry. Moses, in his anger, threw down the tablets and broke them. The Ten Commandments, throughout the history of the world, have been the commandments we have lived by and/or referred to.

We all know the story of the Ten Commandments. God wrote the Ten Commandments on the tablets as His law, which His people were to follow.

Here, God showed His mercy by giving Moses specific instructions on how to rewrite the commandments. When Jehovah gives us specific instructions, we must follow them to the letter. We should not deviate from them. So, when Moses wrote the Ten Commandments as he was instructed this second time, he followed the instructions. Included in God's directions was that he should put the tablets into the ark and carry them with him on his journey.

Finally, Moses was given the city, which was the final place for them to reside. Moses did not question why he closely followed the detailed instructions.

Can we do what God asks of us without questioning why?

When we do and follow the instructions of Jehovah we are assured that we will be victorious. However, when we do not follow the instructions/commandments given there will be potential consequences. In one instance this happened was when Moses did not heed the command of Jehovah was when God told him to speak to the rock to bring forth water for the children of Israel. Moses became angry with the children of Israel because of their constant complaining and struck the rock. God still delivered the water, but because of Moses' disobedience he would not enter into the promise land.

Another story that comes to mind is when God gave specific instructions to Solomon when he was to build a temple for God. God told Solomon the types of materials to use and where to secure them. Solomon even was given the dimensions of how the temple was to be erected. He was told how many men he would need to build the temple, how it was to be dedicated after it was built, and the specific items he was to be put into the temple.

Most of us, while trying to figure out what to do, often make a mess of things. Since owning up to our mistakes is part of a cleansing process, I will include myself.

Because we all are guilty of making a mess of things, whether unintentionally or through actual defiance, I suggest it is easier to trust and not question the leader as we progress with our journey. It is easier to trust and ask no questions. Think of God as being our GPS–God's Plan and Strategy for our lives as he guides us.

The essence of the laws for our lives is the Ten Commandments. First, know that even as we accept these laws, there will be interruptions or bumps in the road. Second, know that the commandments are simplistic–both in how they are worded and in their direct commands. That should make them an easy guide by which to live. When God gives laws to govern our lives, we must follow them.

Read them, they are simplistic, but also quite powerful. Our following them helps us to honor God as well as how we are to treat others. The first four are specific to how we should honor and love God. The remainder are how we should love, treat and honor one another.

Again, Jehovah leaves nothing to chance. Our instructions are clear.

CONSIDER THESE THREE QUESTIONS

1) What is the next assignment?
2) What is it God wants of me?
3) Where do we go from here?

Meditate on the scriptures and the questions. Let this be an important and necessary assignment. But I warn you – do not ask the questions if you are not ready to positively follow the leader. It will be a slow process. But make it steady. Trust Him every step.

Each person's experience will be different but write things down as I did and continue to do so. This is how all the books of the Bible were born. The disciples wrote down His instructions.

SITTING AND LISTENING:

Never give up or give in to the naysayers. Everyone will think they know what is best for you. ONLY GOD KNOWS.

Do not get me wrong, you can listen to others, but then have a conversation with the Master teacher and leader to confirm if what was shared is what He wants for you. We need to listen carefully to others because sometimes the Holy Spirit sends us our messages through others. Life is complicated because, daily we are left to decipher which path we should follow. Daily, we are challenged to try and determine what God is revealing to us. If there are some differences, then you know you must have a discussion with God. If you talk and have daily fellowship with Him and then listen for the next instructions and follow them, you will never be misled and always guided by the Holy Spirit.

Therefore, sitting and/or listening is so important.

REFLECTIONS AND NOTES:

1. Have you ever been given a command by someone in authority to do something, and you had several people in your ear telling you something different or that you should not follow the command? How do you handle such a situation?

2. Many- times, we all will face such a challenge, torn in different directions, trying to please everyone, and forgetting who really is in charge—GOD.

3. Whose commandments and instructions will you follow?

ROOM TO JOURNAL

_____

_____

_____

_____

_____

_____

_____

_____

_____

_____

_____

_____

_____

CHAPTER NINE

"WHAT'S IN YOUR BASKET?"

GOOD FIGS OR BAD FIGS

Jeremiah 24: 2-3- One basket had very good figs, like the figs that are first ripe; and the other basket had bad figs which could not be eaten, they were so bad. Then the Lord said to me "What do you see, Jeremiah?" And I said, " Figs, the good figs, very good; and the bad. Very bad, which cannot be eaten, they are so bad."

Jeremiah 24 (The sign of two baskets of figs) shares an example involving figs. One basket is full of good ripe figs, and the other is full of rotten figs that cannot be eaten. Which basket of figs are you carrying? Are you carrying a basket of good, ripe figs; or are you carrying a basket of rotten, bad figs that should be thrown away?

Jeremiah was charged with delivering the good and the bad news to the children of Israel. It was their choice to listen and decide if they believed that this news came from God, whether to believe it, whether to reject it, and whether this news was sent for them to find the strength to continue their journey.

41

In the Bible, the story in this book of Jeremiah promises that God will set the hearts of the good parts of our lives on Him. Here the commandments, the instructions, the directions and everything that will help us on this journey will be given to us.

The rotten figs can be compared with the residue of disobedience, or what is leftover or washed away. What we do to them can be compared to the consequences of what happens when we are disobedient. The rotten figs are symbolic of those who did not listen. They are symbolic of those who will be taken into an uncomfortable captivity.

Today, the same thing is happening. The worldly order is spinning out of control for some. But not God's world, it is in order. Remember, He never changes, we do.

Again, you should ask yourself, *which basket are you in?*

CONSIDER THIS:

Notes: Compare bad figs to good figs for purposes of friends and choosing friends wisely.

When you compare good figs to bad figs you can distinguish a good friend from a bad friend by the fruit they produce. As in the story good figs are ripe and can be picked an eaten. A good friend can be seen in the same way. They are there for you and will not cause any pain or hurt intentionally. They will always make sure your basket is full of ripe and good fruit that equals good solid friendships.

When we say we have a best friend, what does that really mean? Sometimes, slang refers to "my Betsy," my "BFF." This is someone you share your innermost thoughts with, and someone who will not share those thoughts with anyone else. They will take your innermost thoughts and hold them with respect.

In the dictionary, a "friend" is defined as a person with whom you have a bond or share mutual affection. Typically, this person is in addition to, or exclusive to family. Sometimes, we refer to a family member as our best friend and, often, a spouse is referred to as a best friend.

We might go so far as to refer to the person you hold in high regard as a 'true" friend; they have your back no matter what. They watch out for you and ensure you are not in danger. They will never purposely lead you into making decisions that are not good for you. A true friend will always have your best interest at heart.

Unfortunately, the other side of loyalty is betrayal. It usually involves a circumstance where you find out about the betrayal quite by accident. This is unfortunate because it turns out the person was not your friend. This can be compared to the bad figs that are rotten, and not good for the picking or eating. When you compare this to a friend, this can be a bad influence on you where the rotten fruit can be transferred to you in how you think or treat others because of bitterness. You become bitter and there is no sweetness in the friendship bearing rotten fruit.

If the person is jealous or envious or tries to compete with you, then that becomes the truth of the situation, and although it hurts, you need to walk away because the trust has been broken. Forgive the betrayal because forgiveness lightens your load, and as time goes by let the circumstance be a distant memory.

This is an exercise where you may need to examine your current friendships. If something has been bothering you, follow your gut. This can cut both ways. Are you that friend who feels like you are going to fall away?

SIT AND LISTEN:

Consider yourself and answer these questions:

1) Do you know how to pick a friend based on their fruit?

2) Are they a best friend?

3) Are they an acquaintance?

4) Or do you consider them an associate?

5) How long have you known them?

6) What have you been through together?

7) What have you noticed about them when the going gets tough?

8) Is there a change in behavior when things get difficult?

9) Are their answers encouraging or discouraging?

10) Do their words speak of compliments or criticism?

11) Why is this person in my life right now?

12) Have I been a good friend?

Do not be hard but do be realistic in your assessment. Follow your gut and realize there are times and seasons. Just as the Bible tells us, we may have seasons where people are coming in and out of our lives. We cannot be discouraged by change. Nothing is affixed for a lifetime. So, do not get too deep in this exercise where it becomes unnecessarily distracting.

Two suggestions of songs you may want to listen to are the old spiritual song, "What a Friend We Have in Jesus" by Joseph Scriven and Charles Converse, or "I Am a Friend Of God" by Israel Houghton. Alternately, you may have your own music in mind.

REFLECTION AND NOTES:

If you did the exercise and answered the questions in this chapter, you should now be able to identify what you consider a good or bad friend and what kind of friend you are. Are you a friend that will stick closer than a brother?

ROOM TO JOURNAL

_____

_____

_____

_____

_____

_____

_____

_____

_____

_____

_____

_____

_____

CHAPTER TEN

"DID YOU DO THE PREP WORK?"

1 Kings 10 (Queen of Sheba Praise of Solomon) asks,
"Did you do the prep for the work you have to do?"

T he Queen of Sheba heard that King Solomon of Israel was doing incredible things. Not ready to believe what she had heard she decided to go and see with her own eyes. God led her to do the prep work where she prepared hard questions to ask of Solomon during their meeting. Solomon was able to answer all the questions set forth.

Many times, on our own we do not want to believe what we hear, so we want to verify the information for ourselves. We all have done it, and if we are honest, we still fall into this trap of unbelief. But this chapter/scripture speaks to belief/blessings/honor and wisdom that only God can give. He does this when we have faith and trust Him to rule over our lives.

WHOSE REPORT WILL YOU BELIEVE?

When we listen and obey God's Word, there will be no need to verify any reports. He has the final report on every situation. We will not need to hear or see anything, just believe and have faith even when we cannot see it. People today will question you when you are able to grasp difficult conditions or situations or circumstances. Sometimes our wisdom and discernment must be proven or shown to others before they will believe us.

Let them question you, stick to what you believe and let God speak for you. He will tell you exactly what to say, how to say it, where to say it, and to whom to say it to. He did not say it would be easy, because many times, when you speak the truth, people will question your abilities about the wisdom of God. It is totally interesting how people will show they disagree with you outwardly but deep down inside, or in a private moment, they might admit admiration for your bravery.

I will share something that happened to me many years ago, in my professional career.

I always liked trying to figure out how to improve processes. Whether improving our service, gathering data, or making anything related to our job easier, I liked to make things more efficient. gather information and data.

However, the environment I worked in was not conducive to this. The environment was filled with drama, confusion and chaos. At times, it seemed like watching people run around and around on their life-sized hamster wheel. After sitting in frequent meetings for years, I realized that work was like a soap opera. Same issues, same problems and same characters. Nothing ever progressed.

After observing this repetitive behavior of committee after committee forming to solve the same problem, I had enough. Pushing against the resistance of the company, I started to make a change in my department. Implementing new procedures and modernizing our techniques, we began to improve the efficiency of data flow. At first, I was criticized. many people did not want to change what had "worked" for so many years.

I think it is important to note that I pushed so hard because I felt God telling me it was time to step forward and make a change. After some time, my ideas began to stick. Meetings were shorter and productive, information was shared efficiently, and the company began to work so much better. I was able to achieve that by following what God put in my heart and mind even though it was viewed as wrong and different. I didn't do anything extreme or different. I just did the prep work.

At first, I was criticized because often people do not like change. But in my heart and mind, God was saying it was time to step forward. I thought I was missing out all this time, but in fact, I was progressing by doing things *differently*. Slowly things began to take shape. No more were the meetings overlong, no longer sitting at the table in these big elaborate nonproductive meetings and settings. Do not get me wrong. Sometimes you have to sit in those unproductive meetings but, with what I taught you, you do not have to get stuck at the table.

Just as Solomon gained the wisdom and knowledge by preparing himself with the wisdom of God, you can too.

Follow God's agenda. Sometimes you must tear up people's agendas and bravely start over. Remember, being brave means not using man's agenda, but God's. Do the prep work.

CONSIDER THIS:

When you get invited to sit at the table, will you be prepared? Preparation is the key to success. What is God preparing for you to do?

As a student, you complete the required homework, and you study to prepare yourself for the next semester or grade. You study by yourself or with a group, you may pray together, or prefer to spend time with Jehovah alone. You seek guidance to get clarification or ask for the best direction in which to go. Listening to these instructions will help you become a follower and eventually a leader.

A good example of listening carefully and following instructions and receiving this information as constructive is the example of a young man who had auditioned the year before on a singing show competition but was eliminated. He took the advice of the judges from the previous year, went home, prepared himself through practice, and came back a second time to the competition.

The important thing to know here is that he was not sure where he was in the process. His coming back showed bravery and focus.

Do not ever be defeated. When it is your season, you will sit at the table, stand at the microphone, know that your turn will come, no matter where you are in your process of preparation. Just allow God to be the driving force and come back to the table.

SIT AND LISTEN:

1. Where are you in this season of your life?

2. What is going on in this season? What is going on around you?

3. Of the things that are going on, what can you control?

As I sit amid this season of my life, there are many things going on with or around me, but I have no control of any of it. Both of my hips need replacement surgery. Then, there's the pandemic that the entire world is fighting.

So, I prayed and asked God for guidance. That led me to the right doctor for me. After a series of X-Rays, he immediately said how shocked he was that I even had been able to move the way I was. He recommended surgery and showed me how the culprit was arthritis. Both of my hips had been ravaged. My mother had arthritis, but I had forgotten that hereditary issue. As I wrote this, my first surgery went wonderfully. All the arthritis damage was "chiseled" out of the hip, down to the smallest amount of inflammation. I have had a slow and steady healing process. A physical therapy three times a week has helped. My second surgery also took place during this pandemic. It also was successful as the first one. By following His instructions and listening, God has told me that I will walk upright again and enjoy the rest of my retirement. God has allowed me to embrace this season in my life and to use this time to spend in His presence as I listened for His still voice to speak.

Whatever season you are in, embrace it, learn from it, come out of it a better you, whether it is a physical or spiritual transformation or both. Know that God is in full control.

Prepare yourself for your next season. It is coming. Read Ecclesiastes 3, and know that everything has its time and season. Write yours down as you sit and listen.

REFLECTIONS AND NOTES

1. Remember, no matter the season you are in, preparation will be the key to a successful outcome.

2. Ask yourself daily are you prepared for the day ahead?

3. How do you prepare for your day?

ROOM TO JOURNAL

_____

_____

_____

_____

_____

_____

_____

_____

_____

_____

_____

_____

_____

_____

CHAPTER ELEVEN

"YOU ASK A QUESTION, I WILL TELL YOU NO LIE"

John 8:32- And you will know the truth, and the truth will set you free.

When others question you, and you try to answer them, it may not be what they want to hear. It might be that they do not want to understand or pretend that they cannot comprehend or even know what you are talking about.

Some go so far as to test you, hoping to trip you up. Doesn't that get under your skin? You may raise your hand real high as I do, and, in your mind, you may wonder, "Who do they think they are, questioning me?"

Can you imagine how Jesus must have felt having to defend himself, even after all the miracles and healings the people witnessed. If not, read Mark, 10.

Mark records several instances when the Pharisees question what Jesus is saying and what He advises. Jesus would gather together with a crowd and teach them. The first question the Pharisees asked in Mark 10 was about divorce. Testing Jesus, they asked him if he thought it was lawful for a man to divorce his wife.

Jesus did not get angry. He remained calm and referenced the law from the Old Testament and Moses. As he frequently did, he responded to their question with a question of His own.

"What did Moses command you?"

They said that Moses permitted them to write a certificate of divorce and dismiss her. Jesus went on to say,

"Because of the hardening of your hearts, Moses wrote a precept."

Jesus never wavered in His answers, with either the Pharisees or the disciples. Marriage as it was given in the Bible is a union where two become one, so there is no separation or divorce in the sight of God, and if it is done, then adultery is committed.

So it is that we must remain calm and never waiver in our answers.

As we mature into adulthood, we learn that avoiding anger or strife by changing our words leads to chaos. We may choose not to address a wrong, rebuke a friend, or stand firm on the truth because we want to avoid strife. But oftentimes, this desire to avoid strife will actually create it. We must stand firm and defend the truth of the Word.

I will pause here for a minute, as the Holy Spirit speaks to me. Now, I ask you, "Can you follow this instruction with a child-like spirit?"

Jesus made it clear what is required to enter the kingdom. As he teaches in the beginning of Mark chapter 10, to humble ourselves as children, we are commanded to love one another as He loves us with compassion. Give freely to those in need, and do not store up the riches of the world.

The innocence in a child's eyes see no color, hate, racism, anger, or displays distrustful traits. Children possess the purest hearts and have no preconceived notions or thoughts. The purity and innocence of life is seen in their playful spirit to run and explore life seen through the eyes of God with laughter and joy.

However, as adults, our eyes have been open to the many things of life: hate, racism, anger, distrust, and disappointment. The good news is as we navigate through the different experiences, we can look through the lens of God's eye: who will show us his unconditional love, leading us in following His instructions.

CONSIDER THIS ANALOGY:

There is no escaping the truth of God's Word. As He reminds us in John 15, we must allow Him to abide is us as he abides in His Father.

There was a game show in the late 1950s and early 1960s called, "To Tell the Truth." It recently has been resurrected with the principal format of a celebrity panel questioning contestants to determine who the actual person is. They must determine who has done something important, or stakes a claim to a certain thing or invention. The game is about discovering who is telling the truth.

The panel of three must make this determination based on the three contestant's answers.

Now as this came to mind, when people ask who you are, do you tell the truth, or are you an imposter and tell a lie or pretend to be someone else? Ask yourself are you truthful and honest with yourself first so you can then be honest with others.

Check yourself daily, ask God to check your heart daily, and be reminded that you must be true to your own self.

Society might tempt you, making you think that telling the truth is a painful chore for most, and that a *little white lie* is better to appease others or to keep from hurting someone's feelings.

It is better not to try to escape God's Word. Worship Him in spirit and in truth. If you do this, you will have nothing to remember in your daily entanglements.

SIT AND LISTEN:

A Prayer

Please open our eyes of understanding to see you, God, as a little child sees with humility, the spirit of love, and seeing beyond the naked eye into the spirit realm. Our eyes are the gateway and light to our spirit.

Matthew 6:22

"The lamp of the body is the eye, therefore if your eye is good your hold body will be full of light."

REFLECTION AND NOTES:

1. How do you allow the light of God to radiate through your eyes and shine?

2. How do you handle those who always question what you say or your credibility?

ROOM TO JOURNAL

_____

_____

_____

_____

_____

_____

_____

_____

_____

_____

_____

_____

_____

CHAPTER TWELVE

"ABIDING WITH GOD/ REVEALING HIS TRUTH"

John15:1-5

"I am the true vine, and My Father is the vinedresser. Every branch in Me that does not bear fruit He takes away; and every branch that bears fruit He prunes that it may bear more fruit. You are already clean because of the word which I have spoken to you. Abide in Me, and I in you. As the branch cannot bear fruit of itself, unless it abides in the vine, neither can you, unless you abide in Me. " I am the vine, you are the branches. He who abides in Me, and I in him, bears much fruit; for without Me you can do nothing,

When the Holy Spirit places a scripture in your heart, and you are familiar with it, many times we think we already know what God is trying to say or convey to us. This happened to me this morning, and I had to push the reset button and start all over reading this scripture and ask the Holy Spirit to speak to my heart as Jesus spoke in this scripture.

I began to read John, chapter 15, and the word entangled came to me.

When I first looked at the scripture, I found myself having to read it several times to understand how it was relevant to me. Then the light bulb went off. In John 15, Jesus speaks about the vine and branches He compares Himself to being the vine. His Father is the vinedresser, and we are the branches who are entangled together. Verse two reminds us that every branch does not bear fruit. We, the branches, can only produce fruit if we receive nourishment from the Father.

The problem with trees is sometimes they require pruning. Pruning involves clipping and trimming parts of the tree's branches dead or alive that would prohibit the branches from producing fruit. The same is for us. God prunes us – removing memories, sins, or thoughts that would keep us from bearing fruit. while doing that He gently reminds us that if we abide in Him, He will abide in us.

There is also a warning. Jesus explains that if we do not abide in Him, if we reject being entangled with him – we will be withered up and cast into a fire and burned up. If this sounds drastic, think of how you may burn dead limbs when cleaning a garden. However, it is very easy to avoid this, we simply must choose to be fruitful by abiding in Him. When you do this, you are put in a place to glorify God and allow Him to manifest in your life. You will produce good fruit.

CONSIDER THIS
SIT AND LISTEN

Truth brings freedom and breaks the chains of bondage that keep us bound when we do not want to hear the truth or respect the truth or receive the true and living word from God.

What chains have you in bondage from receiving the truth about your life?

Take a moment and ask yourself this question. It may be difficult, but be truthful, but it will start the ball rolling.

I asked myself the question and had to accept some of my past's indiscretions that had me in chains and shackles.

I repented and asked Jehovah to help me walk out of my past guilt and shame and restore me and renew my mind, and my spirit to see me as He sees me.

I have allowed Him to love on me and I love Him. In this quiet time together, I can hear Him, so to speak, and I listen for His holy instructions. This is a process, in spending quality time with Him. Do not get discouraged, it will take time.

I am still a work in progress, threading the needle and starting the sewing process, trying to stay entwined in the vines and the branches. I warn you it will take practice, practice, and more practice.

REFLECTIONS AND NOTES

What are you trying to escape from in your life that you need to tackle head on?

ROOM TO JOURNAL

_____

_____

_____

_____

_____

_____

_____

_____

_____

_____

_____

_____

CHAPTER FOURTEEN

"THE BEATITUDES/ THE BLESSINGS"

Matthew 5:3-12

- *Blessed are the poor in spirit for theirs is the Kingdom of Heaven.*

- *Blessed are those that mourn for they shall comforted.*

- *Blessed are the meek for they shall inherit the earth.*

- *Blessed are those who hunger and thirst for righteousness, for they shall be filled.*

- *Blessed are the merciful, for they shall be shown mercy.*

- *Blessed are the pure in heart for they shall see God.*

- *Blessed are the peacemakers for they will be called the children of God.*

- *Blessed are those who are persecuted because of righteousness, for theirs is the Kingdom of Heaven.*

In Matthew 5:3-12, Jesus shares the Beatitudes with the people. The Beatitudes, a part of His Sermon on the Mount, describe the blessings of those who have certain qualities or experiences particular to those belonging to the kingdom of Heaven. It is easy to remember when we know that BEATI and SUNT together mean "Blessed Are," The latin translation of BEATUS means "happy" and "blessed".

The Beatitudes seem to offer various consolations to the downtrodden. While Jesus sets forth these lessons in humility, we can receive them as stern standards of how we will be judged and go on to receive them as strict guidance leading us in how we should conduct ourselves and behave when helping others in need.

Do you accept them as blessings, consolation, or standards by which we will be judged?

The Beatitudes as found in Matthew 5:3-12 are as follows:

- *Blessed are the poor in spirit for theirs is the Kingdom of Heaven.*

- *Blessed are those that mourn for they shall comforted.*

- *Blessed are the meek for they shall inherit the earth.*

- *Blessed are those who hunger and thirst for righteousness, for they shall be filled.*

- *Blessed are the merciful, for they shall be shown mercy.*

- *Blessed are the pure in heart for they shall see God.*

- *Blessed are the peacemakers for they will be called the children of God.*

- *Blessed are those who are persecuted because of righteousness, for theirs is the Kingdom of Heaven.*

The Holy Spirit tells us we critically need all of these attributes today.

Our world is not at peace. Anger and hate for one another continue to be fueled by over four hundred years of the demonic spirit of slavery.

Our world is in turmoil, confusion, chaos, hate. It is driven by the history of racism, divisiveness, self-centered leaders, selfishness, killing, and more. Because of your skin color, police have no regard for life. Again, that does not pertain to all. All of these problems have the COVID-19 pandemic as a catalyst.

We are challenged to not just care more about what people are going to say and think more about telling the truth. The word of God is simplistic, but powerful. The instructions are clear as to what is required of us who know Him. The pandemic has fueled a time and season where the healthy thing to do is to refrain from one another by wearing masks and practicing social distancing.

Do not be afraid to be the force that brings the world healing power.

The saying goes, if you do not learn the lesson, history will repeat itself.

> "My philosophy is if you don't study for the test,
> you will fail the test and have to take the class all
> over again."

When we allow ourselves to maintain meekness, peacefully review the past, seek positive change, and practice the Beatitudes, we will have the fortitude to go forward to affect change on the earth.

There will be judgment for not doing what Jehovah requires of us. Follow the blueprint given at the Sermon on the Mount and live it daily in your witness to who God is in you.

Jehovah has set a standard for us to live by, are you? When you miss the mark, repent, ask forgiveness, and get back on the journey.

In the Beatitudes, we are promised that the meek will inherit the earth. We are asked to be peacemakers so that we will be called the children of God. But here, we must know that being "meek" or a "peacemaker" does not mean shrinking from our fight about what is best for the greater good.

Being meek or humble, quiet, gentle, and easily imposed does not mean we have to be submissive or what some people might think is being a pushover.

In the Biblical context, "meek" is a person who is not continually concerned with His own ways, ideas, or wishes. They are willing to put their own needs second and submit to others to achieve what is good for others.

2 Chronicles 7:14 supports Matthew 5 by asking us to bring healing to the land. To paraphrase the scripture, it starts off by asking people who are called by His name to humble themselves and pray and seek His face. The scripture further asks that we turn from our wicked ways, hear from heaven, and be forgiven for sins while Jesus heals our land.

Do not be afraid to be different. If you are still and listen, He will tell you and show you what you need to know and do. Will you be able to handle it and receive it?

Will you be able to make the necessary changes required to have a meek and peaceful spirit to bring calm to a hurting world?

HOW CAN I DO THIS?

Start with a small gesture—checking on the elderly, offering to get groceries, or do the yard or laundry. You may choose something else you see that is needed in your community. Let the gesture grow.

We can change the world with one kind gesture at a time.

CONSIDER THIS: IN 2020 the World faced a pandemic that shut down the entire world. Everyone was under mandatory lock downs to stop the spread of COVID-19, Many lost love ones, friends, jobs, and social injustice rose to a level of contention as people of color were killed at the hands of police. Protest for justice rang from the four corners of the earth amid a pandemic.

Ask Jehovah what was I to learn from this? What were your initial thoughts and what are your thoughts now?

Compare notes and take inventory. Make sure you consolidate the list.

Blessings can still come out of a crisis or a conflict. Many will think I am crazy to say this, but it is true. Even in this pandemic, there are blessings to be found. You may say, "Such as?" Those who have learned the lesson and passed the test will have a kinder and gentler spirit as they look for the blessings.

Look for peacemakers, look for followers and leaders, look for humility, look at tests that have been studied, and tests that have been passed, look for humility to emerge and in these prominent positions that in effect change the world, look for Jehovah as He changes this world into one, we have never seen and will probably never see again in our lifetime.

Yes, we have lost many along the journey, but their legacy has been the catalyst to shift the world and bring about the change. Change is difficult when you do not want to change, but easy when you allow Jehovah to make the change in you. This is the path of least resistance. Now for those who decide they do not want to shift and change all I will say is you missed an opportunity of a lifetime.

The choices you make today will affect every decision you make forever.

SIT AND LISTEN:

Lyrics are so appropriate – for instance, consider the song, "Everything Must Change" by Bernard Igher.

I listened to the version sung by George Benson and I wept, because we must allow change to grow in us, or we will never see the full potential of God in us.

My prayer for everyone is that you listen to these lyrics or any song that speaks of change and see the beauty and necessity of making whatever changes you need to get to the next level of your Journey.

REFLECTION AND NOTES:

Considering the questions in this chapter, ask yourself:

1. Where am I?
2. Where do I need to go?

ROOM TO JOURNAL

_____

_____

_____

_____

_____

_____

_____

_____

_____

_____

_____

_____

_____

CHAPTER FIFTEEN

"FORGIVENESS IS THE KEY"

Psalm 39: 1-3-I said, " I will guard my ways, Lest I sin with my tongue; I will restrain my mouth with a muzzle, While the wicked are before me," I was mute with silence, I held my peace even from good; And my sorrow was stirred up. My heart was hot within me; While I was mussing, the fire burned. Then I spoke with my tongue.

In Psalm 39, we find that forgiveness is the key. But Jehovah also shared with me simultaneously the word *wisdom*—wisdom plus forgiveness? These are two of the most significant words that are instructions on how we should govern and live on this earth.

Defining these two words and living them are two different things. You know, we all know what something may mean, but do we apply it to everyday living, as we should.

Let us look at the biblical definition of wisdom. In 1 Corinthians 12:8, wisdom is presented as a spiritual gift.

The root word *wise*—is to have understanding and knowledge that goes beyond the realm of how we think. And it is important to know how Jehovah thinks and shares wisdom with us via the Holy Spirit. We can call this "Spiritual Wisdom." Wisdom that goes beyond knowing, a wisdom that knows how to apply the knowledge that Jehovah has imparted into our everyday living. An ability to discern when to apply it, and it adds up to a wisdom that Jehovah allows us as the key to open the gates to understand his godly wisdom.

Not everybody will have the listening ear to hear the spiritual wisdom of Jehovah to receive this gift. However, if this gift is bestowed upon you, share it wisely as God allows you to.

Forgiveness is a word that can change your life forever. It is a principle or concept that many struggles with daily. We all have been hurt, disappointed, abused, neglected or misunderstood, verbally abused, emotionally abused, and even physically abused; or you have been the one who did these hurtful things to someone.

Forgiveness is the ability to step out of our prideful ways and step into a place where we can show humility and say we are "Sorry." For many, saying *I am sorry* is difficult. But being able to truly be sorry is powerful and it can heal wounds that have been festering for years. The irony is the wounds I am talking about are the cumulative circumstances in our lives that may not be related to what we call wounds but are the pain we feel in our hearts. You get the picture, right?

These are areas in our lives where many times, we cannot bring ourselves to forgive a person or ask for forgiveness because we are chained and shackled and in bondage ourselves.

Jesus said it on the cross, *"Forgive them Father, for they know no not what they do."*

Even in His pain and suffering, He asked that the people be forgiven for what they had done. Consider the power of His forgiveness.

Many times, in our lives people will hurt you and not even realize it. That is why it is important to let them know they hurt you so you can forgive them. Forgiveness sets you free from the pain and hurt. The final ingredient to the "forgiveness victory" is throwing it into the sea of forgetfulness.

This can and will be a bitter pill for many to swallow, but true forgiveness and breaking those chains and shackles is freeing.

The Apostle Paul reminds us to forget those things behind us and to press ahead to the mark of the calling of Jesus. Consider that whatever God wants to do in our lives might be driven by forgiveness as the key. It might be the key to opening your heart to let Jesus in. It is the main key to opening the door to your destiny, purpose, and plan for your life.

Remember, when we forgive, it is not for the other person. Forgiveness is for us, to become free from pain and hurt. And if we need to ask for forgiveness, it also frees us from the pain and hurt that we may have caused someone else.

In Psalm 39, David gives us the blueprint of how we can obtain the wisdom to ask for forgiveness. He reminds us that God's wisdom is knowing when to speak and when to be quiet.

When you open yourself up to God, even after being silent while discerning His wisdom, as you cry out asking for forgiveness of your transgressions and you are sincere and faithful that God will restore your strength, you will receive wisdom beyond your years and understanding.

CONSIDER THIS:

"Say, I am SORRY."

For what are you SORRY? Begin with the issue of not being able to say the word "sorry" when you needed to.

To whom have you had to say SORRY? Anyone, who shares your life or everyone, you might have to say you are sorry to people you do not know and have yet to meet probably because of something unkind you have said.

Why did you have to say you were Sorry? Free all who you may have hurt or offended knowingly and unknowingly.

Why haven't you said, I am SORRY?

Hopefully, this will spark the fire in your heart to prepare a list of those to whom you need to say you are SORRY.

Ask yourself if it is too late for you to ask for forgiveness or to forgive? If you find yourself where others do not want to forgive you and accept your apology, consider if you are finding it hard to forgive others?

Go to God in prayer and release it to Him. Let Him deal with the situation. Forgiveness is the ability to step out of our prideful ways.

Some of us might need to do this as a verbal exercise. We may need to reach out to the person to whom we need to say, I am SORRY. This may be difficult. Keep praying, asking for guidance on how you can proceed with humility, and eventually, the word, "Sorry" will be easier. It can heal wounds that have been open for years. You get the picture, right?

Now consider that two-way communication comes in two primary forms, it may be verbal or written.

A) Verbally means speak with the person face-to-face or even by phone. Face-to-face is harder. Never force anyone to meet you. If you can meet with the person, you may ask if you can bring someone with you for moral support and minimize any tension of having a face-to-face. Over the phone is easier. But do not take the easiest way out.

B) My mother used to say write a letter, sleep on it, and basically, by reading it, you will discover it easier to send the letter. If you feel comfortable, remember when sending it by mail, you must feel the same way by the time it is received. If you email it, make sure careful wording expresses your emotions and intent. Technology allows us to communicate faster with people all around the globe.

This is an exercise that I did, and if you are true to yourself, you must carefully choose which is best—in person, by phone, writing by snail mail, or by email. You may have to do this numerous times to find the best way.

You may have an issue with pride. You may be harboring an unforgiving spirit. We must be true to ourselves.

Start slow, acknowledge you have an issue with saying you are sorry, and acknowledge if you find it difficult to forgive others or yourself. This is the first step to starting the healing process.

You may need to seek professional help if the situation is too complicated to help you navigate through this terrain. Years ago, counseling was not considered helpful, but in this complicated and noisy world, counseling is a good place to start.

Whether you pray, or do not pray "the Lord's Prayer," found in Matthew 6: 9-15. It is always a good place to start.

"Our Father who art in heaven, hallowed be thy name. Thy Kingdom Come. Thy will be done in earth as it is heaven. Give us this day our daily bread. And forgive us our debts, as we forgive our debtors. And lead us not into temptation but deliver us from evil: For Thine is the kingdom, and the power, and the glory, forever. Amen."

Try these scriptures on forgiveness:

Ephesians 4: 31-32 speaks of getting rid of bitterness, rage, anger, brawling and slander, and other forms of malice. Be kind and compassionate to one another, forgiving each other, just as in Christ, God forgave you.

The Lord's Prayer is an instruction that, when followed, tells us to forgive other people when they sin against you, your heavenly Father will also forgive you. If you do not forgive others of their sins, your Father will not forgive you of your sins.

WHAT IS THE ACRONYM TO FORGIVENESS?

F- Faith/Freedom- when you forgive yourself and others
O- Obedience- brings forgiveness to yourself and others
R- Repent- of your sins when you forgive yourself and others
G- Goodness/Grace of Jesus -when you forgive yourself and others
I- Internal- forgiveness brings peace to oneself
V- Victory in Jesus when you forgive
N- Notify- those you are forgiving
E- Everlasting Peace when you forgive
S- Surrender to Jesus- it allows forgiveness

S- Salvation- you are safe in His arms when you forgive.

SIT AND LISTEN:

Always be able to forgive yourself. Never be too big to ask for forgiveness or forgive others so God can forgive you. Never be too big to say you are sorry. Remember the key is never look back when we have said we are sorry. When we have asked for forgiveness, throw the pain and hurt into the sea of forgetfulness. Truly mean it in your heart, so it will release the chains and shackles and free you from the bondage of pain and hurt. It starts with the powerful words, "I AM SORRY."

REFLECTIONS AND NOTES:

Reference the thought in this chapter and ask yourself:

1. What are the attributes that I contribute to true forgiveness?

2. What does true forgiveness mean to you?

ROOM TO JOURNAL

CHAPTER SIXTEEN

"RESET OR PAUSE"

*If I asked you to reset or pause your phone, which one
will you hit?*

As you may know, the Psalms are divided into five
books consisting of 150 Psalms. When the Spirit led
me to read book 4 of the Psalms 90-106. This book focuses
on how God is above us. In Psalm 90 records simultaneously
asking God to be merciful on His people while acknowledging that God is eternally powerful.

In Moses' prayer, he also acknowledges the sins
of the people and the anger of Jehovah. He did not
make excuses for the people, rather, he asked for wisdom and
understanding. Knowing that God had turned away from
them because of their sin, he pleaded with God to turn
back to His people and give them another chance. God listened. Despite their disobedience, he showed them mercy.

He allowed both a reset (start over) button to be
hit as well as a PAUSE button as Moses cried out to
Jehovah, acknowledging He is God who made the
Earth, and this is His world.

Also, the children of Israel had sinned against Him, they repented, and God had mercy on them, and He established them, and the beauty of the Lord our God (acknowledging Him) was upon their hands and the works of their hands established thou it. Meaning everything they touched would be blessed.

When a child does something wrong his/her parents have to discipline. This discipline is not because the parents are cruel and unloving but rather they don't want to see their child go astray, Now, I want to speak to those who may not have had a mom or dad.

Jehovah wanted me to remind you your biological parents may have conceived you, but He created you and loves you unconditionally. No strings attached.

When He loves you, He will correct you, in love.

CONSIDER THIS:

Usually, when we do a reset, we are starting over or are given the opportunity for a do-over. This may be a necessary action to correct something or re-order our steps on our life journey for God's plan to go forward. To "pause" and reflect, take a moment to access where we are in a process may be necessary to rearrange somethings before we continue along the path.

God reminds us he is still in charge but as the world dealt with the COV-19 Pandemic, we may need to take this time to pause. For some of us, we might take the time to do a reset. The words "reset" and "pause" are the key to us at this time to reflect and make the necessary changes in our journey.

Either it was a time for us and the world to hit the RESET button in our lives and start anew or PAUSE where you are at and take inventory. Only you and God know what this would mean to you and for you.

For me, I needed to hit the reset button and renew my relationship with Jehovah, spending quality time, not just anytime. I needed to assess my current relationships and determine if the season for some of these relationships were over as I currently knew them. Or, that they were over, period. Maybe it was time to let them fade to black. Now I know this has been a struggle for me to let go, but in one instance, one of my friendships was taken away from me during the pandemic, not by COVID-19, but the person passed away of natural causes. This person was blocking me from moving on and making decisions about whether they could be more than a friend in my life and opening to new, other possibilities. God had a plan, and He had already given me the new a possibility, several months before the pandemic hit and the reset button had been hit. I went with the new start-over. The person is exactly what God knew I needed and desired, and He is the best, kind, loving, and compassionate man I have ever met.

So now, what is it you need to reset in your life? This is the time to do it while you are not doing the hustling and running around just existing. Now is the time to be still to listen to the inner voice to know you need to reset something specific in your life and start fresh

Even if you didn't have the opportunity to do this during the pandemic, the exercise is a good one now to put it in your arsenal, so when life is heavy or you are experiencing something difficult, it would be a good time to ask God if it is an appropriate time to hit the reset button and ask God for instructions on how to proceed.

Follow the instructions. The reset will be amazing, beyond what you could ever imagine.

For some, the PAUSE button may be the more appropriate button you need to hit.

When we pause, it usually means you are doing something or started something and you have to stop to do something else or address something else immediately before you can go back to where you were, not necessarily requiring going back to the beginning, but resuming where you are in the process or need to have a do-over before you continue on.

Sometimes in life we must pause, reflect on where we are, what we are doing and determine if we are on the right path, or need to reassess if we have made some mistakes that require our attention to correct.

When I looked up the definition, it is to *interrupt an action,* or a temporary stop.

If you see where God is taking us during this time, the keys are knowing the appropriate actions necessary to hit the pause button. As I said earlier, a do-over action may be required at the point you hit the pause button. Again, this will be a pivotal moment in your life, knowing the appropriate action(s) to take before you release the pause button to continue. Follow the instructions you receive.

What comes to mind is when you hit the pause button on a DVD player, there can be a few reasons: you need to go to the bathroom, or you need to answer the telephone, or the doorbell rings, you need to get the popcorn out of the microwave.

Because we don't want to lose our place, or we don't want to miss any part or scene in the movie or show.

Now with that in mind, if you decided you needed to hit the PAUSE button or Jehovah hits the PAUSE button for you, what is it you will need to do to release the pause.

For me it was, to look at my actions, to see if they lined up with what God wanted of me and make the necessary adjustments, He required so He could release the pause button to continue my life's journey.

SIT AND LISTEN:

Be still. Whether you hit the reset button or the pause button, just relax and let Jehovah guide you through the process. Again, a restart may require several steps and actions. Prayer, reading His word, forgiveness, etc. Whatever it requires, do not shy away, embrace the journey whether you hit the reset or God hit it. Just follow the leader and watch where He will take you.

I promise you, you will enjoy the ride, but I didn't say it wouldn't present some challenges along the way, even embrace them, as they will strengthen you.

Now for the pause button, a do-over at a point and time, in some instances, this will truly present challenges, because usually you are in the process and any changes could take you back to having to consider a reset. I said it as Jehovah gives it. So, remember follow the instructions even if it means releasing the PAUSE button and hitting the RESET button. God knows just what button you will need to hit and the appropriate time.

For those who think you will never have to do this, think again. Keep living and get your hand ready.

Out of your obedience comes the blessing, even as you hit the bumps in the road.

REFLECTIONS AND NOTES:

1. *When have you hit a reset or pause button in your life? What was going on in your life at that time.*

2. *Assess what changed during that time in your life. Who came in and out of your life*

ROOM TO JOURNAL

_____

_____

_____

_____

_____

_____

_____

_____

_____

_____

_____

_____

_____

_____

_____

Chapter Seventeen

"Handling An Encounter"

*John 4: 7-10-A woman of Samaria came to draw water.
Jesus said to her, "Give Me a drink. For His disciples had
gone away into the city to buy food. Then the woman of
Samaria said to Him, " How is it that You, being a Jew, ask
a drink from me, a Samaritan woman?" For Jews have no
dealings with Samaritans. Jesus answered and said to her, " If
you knew the gift of God, and who it is who says to you, " Give
Me a drink, you would have asked him, and He would
have given you living water."*

How would you handle an encounter? You may
ask, *What kind of encounter?* My answer is any kind
of encounter whether anticipated or unanticipated. How you
handle it might determine the next steps on your journey.

Let us look at what happened when the Samaritan
women met the Messiah in John 4. Jesus was traveling
through Samaria and took a moment to rest next to a
well. As he is resting, a Samaritan woman came to
draw water and has an encounter with Jesus at
the well. As she approached, Jesus said.

"Give me a drink of water,"

The Samaritan woman was surprised. At that time, Jews avoided any interaction with Samaritans. As she regains her composure she asked why he addressed her. Jesus replied.

"If you knew the gift of God and who it is who says, 'give me a drink,' you would have asked Him and He would have given you living water."

"Sir," she replied, "you have nothing to draw the water and the well is deep.

Jesus replied.

"Whoever drinks of this water will thirst again, but whoever drinks of the water I give will be from a fountain of water springing up into everlasting life and they will never thirst again."

After listening to Jesus, the Samaritan woman wanted to know how she could drink and never thirst again and never have to come back to this well.

After He explained to her what He meant, He asked her to bring her husband, but she replied.

"I have no husband."

"You have had five husbands and the one you are with now is not your husband, in that you spoke truly."

Now knowing that Jesus knew this about her, the women said to Him,

"Sir, I perceive you to be a prophet."

We will often be going about our daily life and suddenly we meet someone that we never expected to meet. It could be someone outside of our usual daily encounters. It could be a famous athlete, an entertainer, an author, or a person we knew, but have not seen or heard from in years. Usually, we are pleasantly surprised. We may embrace the moment and interact, or we may make excuses and avoid them because we are shy or uncomfortable.

WHAT IF YOU HAVE AN ENCOUNTER WITH GOD?

How would you act? Would you introduce yourself and fellowship with Him or shy away? We cannot worry about how we look at this time because God has been watching our every move.

When you encounter those who can speak into your life and tell you things only Jehovah would know, consider it a blessing. Consider that the Holy Spirit might be trying to send you a message, listen carefully and take heed.

"You worship where you do not know. We know what and whom we worship. But the hour is coming and now is when the true worshippers will worship the Father in spirit and in truth."

> "God is a spirit and those who worship Him must do it in "spirit and in truth." The Father is seeking such to worship Him."

The Samaritan women said to Jesus, *I know the Messiah is coming who they call Christ, and when He comes, He will tell us all things. Jesus said to her, I who speak to you am He.*

Can you imagine how the Samaritan woman probably felt? She was speaking with Christ the entire time and did not know it.

What I love about this story after hearing and reading it many times, was that the woman was very transparent and shared her story, and life with a stranger. Yet, she did not realize this encounter would probably change her life forever.

When we are transparent, when we are truthful and honest, when we open our hearts to Jehovah and allow Him to speak to us, our encounters with others and with Jesus can change a situation or circumstance in an instant.

The key is spending quality time in worship with Him, worshipping Him in spirit and truth, and making truth and honesty a key part of our lives.

Worship is a time to give praise and honor to Him and let your spirits flow together. Allow Him to speak to the Holy Spirit, which is your inner voice. Allow Him to give instructions and insight about what you are to do next on your journey.

The Samaritan woman received specific instructions on how she was to worship the Father.

When we have such encounters with Jehovah, do we allow ourselves to receive specific instructions? We cannot take this opportunity lightly. God is trying to tell us something. We must be in tune so our ears will hear, and the transmission will be crystal clear.

This reminds me of the song from the movie, *The Color Purple*," Maybe God is Tryin to Tell You Somethin", by Quincy Jones , Soundtrack from the movie.

Ask yourself, what is God trying to tell you? Are you ready to hear it? Will you listen and follow His instructions to a tee?

SIT AND LISTEN:

Be doers of His Word by following the instructions in James 1:22.

Listen to the lyrics of the song by Donnie McClurkin and let God speak to your heart.

REFLECTION AND NOTES:

1. Think of an encounter that you were not prepared for, how did you handle it?

2. Think of an encounter you had that you were prepared for, how did you handle it?

3. Compare both and look for areas to improve so you can always be prepared. The key to this exercise is to write out the encounters and look at the preparation and steps as a guide for handling future encounters.

4. Also, what is the message GOD is trying to convey to you in the encounter?

ROOM TO JOURNAL

_____

_____

_____

_____

_____

_____

_____

_____

_____

_____

_____

_____

Chapter Eighteen

"The Best Help"

I will lift of my eyes to the hills (God/Jehovah) from which cometh my help. My help cometh from the Lord, who made the heavens and earth. He would not suffer thy foot to be moved; He that keepeth thee will not slumber. Behold, He that keepeth thee shall neither slumber nor sleep. The Lord is thy keeper: The Lord is our shade upon thy right hand. The sun shall not smite thee by day, or the moon by night. The Lord shall preserve thy soul. The Lord shall preserve thy going out and thy coming in from this time forth, and even forever more. Psalms 121

Let us explore this word. Help is defined as doing something by offering one's service or resources. Also, it means serving someone by offering them the food or drink they need, or the action of helping someone and helping do something. When someone helps you, they are giving service in some form or another. We are of this by the simple four-letter word "help." We should not take the word for granted. What does the word *help* mean? What does it truly mean to you?

In the context of our help coming from Jehovah, the word "All" takes it up a notch and a level that no one else can match or compete with.

We do need help and support from those around us and in our lives, daily. But when we recall the old saying, *"When the going gets tough, the tough get going."* God must be tough because He never leaves us.

H- Healing/Humility
E- Enlightenment
L- Love
P – Peace

When we ask for help, it shows that you are open to being healed from what ever you need and you are humble enough to know that you require help. This opens up your heart to be enlightened by knowing you are not alone because the love of Jehovah is showing you that He gives the best help in any situation when you allow him to take over. After which the peace of Jehovah will engulf you and comfort you as his help guides you through your circumstances/situation.

Jehovah wants to serve His children by helping us be the best, achieving the best, and then serving others and helping them to know Him so that they can be the best. Remember to share the gospel, the good news.

The goal is to get us where He has purposed us to be when He created us. Our life had been set.

Now, getting "All your Help" from the Master can lead to our serving others.

CONSIDER THIS:

There is a commercial for a "Life Alert Device."

The elderly lady lies on the floor and says to those listening, "Help I've fallen, and I can't get up." In another marketing scenario, the person has fallen in the bathtub.

They both need help, and the message is that there is no one else in the house to help them. But of course, purchasing the Life Alert Device offers that sense of security that offers help. This is a great thing to have if you are a person who is at risk of falling and live alone.

The help that comes from Jehovah in our time of need is free. Many of us will seek out others for help or things that will require us to pay for help do to our prideful ways that will not allow us to ask for help through prayer. We say, I can do this. I do not need any help from anybody.

We all need help, some more than others. Be honest with yourself and you will be surprised at the sense of relief. All we must do is ask. In Matthew 7:7-8, we find one of our most popular scriptures, *"Ask, and it shall be given you; seek, and ye shall find; knock, and it shall be opened unto you.* All our help Comes from the Lord. There are four things to remember when we open ourselves to HELP from God- Humility/ Healing, Enlightenment, Love and Peace in any situation

SIT AND LISTEN:

1. Where do you turn when you need help? Every time you require help from now on, sit with God and talk to Him about the help you require. Don't try to figure it out on your own. Ask yourself the following:

2. What stems from you needing help? Is it something you did or did not do that requires the help? If repentance is part of getting this help, are you ready to surrender? Can you forgive freely if that is where the help must originate?

Every morning you wake-up, God has helped you be. He is blowing His breath in you and me.

And each new day where he has shown His grace and mercy, you should start with a Hallelujah or thank you!

REFLECTIONS AND NOTES

Look at the acronym of HELP in the chapter and, going forward, incorporate the words Humility/Healing, Enlightenment, Love and Peace. Meditate on these words as you seek help. Then journal how you were guided through the process and the steps taken. I promise the ease of the HELP will amaze you as you allow these four things to take over.

ROOM TO JOURNAL

_____

_____

_____

_____

_____

_____

_____

_____

_____

_____

_____

_____

_____

_____

CHAPTER NINETEEN

"TIME IS OF THE ESSENCE"

What season do you find yourself in?

Procrastination is a word that most of us know all too well. We ponder over if we should do something... should we wait or go full speed ahead? Procrastination is defined as the action of delaying or postponing something.

Ecclesiastes 3 puts time into perspective when it reminds us that there is a time and a season to everything under the sun.

The noun "time" means the indefinite and continued progress of the existence of something, and how long it took it to exist—seconds, minutes, hours, days, weeks, months, years, and so on.

The verb "time" refers to planning, arranging, and scheduling something to occur at a specific hour, on a certain day, and to happen or to be done in a particular month and year.

Solomon is speaking in Ecclesiastes and he reminds us, in verses 1 through 8 that there is a time and season for everything, and we must be prepared and know what time and season we are in. He begins by telling us there is a season for everything. The list that follows and determine your season. While you study the list below, notice that each item has an opposite.

- *A time for every purpose under the heaven.*
- *A time to be born and a time to die.*
- *A time to plant and a time to pluck up what has been planted.*
- *A time to kill and a time heal.*
- *A time to break down and a time to build up.*
- *A time to weep and a time to laugh.*
- *A time mourn and a time to dance.*
- *A time to cast away stones and a time to gather stones.*
- *A time to embrace and a time to refrain.*
- *A time to gain and a time to lose.*
- *A time to keep and a time to throw away.*
- *A time to tear and a time to sew.*
- *A time to keep silence and a time to speak.*
- *A time to love and a time to hate.*
- *A time of war and a time for peace.*

In the early 70s, there was a sitcom called "Good Times" about a family struggling to survive in the ghetto while living in the projects. Times for this family were difficult. Many times the father found himself without a decent job to provide for his family. Because of this, he struggled to keep a roof over their head and put food on the table.

The Evans family always found a way to see the good in every situation no matter how difficult or challenging it was.

They went through different seasons or lessons and they always came out better because they learned as a family.

That is what we need to learn. Whether as a biological or spiritual family, we must find the good even in our most challenging times and seasons. How we choose to handle these difficult times in different seasons in our life are critical to how we grow and learn.

Solomon specifically tells exactly the different seasons we may face but when we encounter these seasons, it is a time, we should embrace it and allow Jehovah to teach us and grow us Spiritually. In these various seasons, which we all will experience, it should be a time to reflect on where we are in our life. We consider the next lesson and wonder what we are supposed to take from this season, as we prepare for our next season.

Many times, when we are going through a difficult time and season, we must be reminded, this too shall pass, but while in it, prepare yourself so when you come through it, you will be a better person for the experience and can help somebody else when they are in a similar season. Praying with and for them, giving an encouraging word or just a listening ear.

The saying is, "It is always the darkest before the dawn," and "After the storm the sun shines bright as if there had been no storm." I added my touch to it.

This brings me to the story where the disciples were on a boat with Jesus, and Jesus was sleeping. A storm came up in the sea and was raging. The disciples became frightened and went to awake Jesus. They cried, "Lord, save us!" "We're going to drown."

Jesus said, "You of little faith. Why are you afraid?"

The scripture goes on to say, He got up and rebuked the winds and the waves and it was completely calm. The disciples were amazed, asking what kind of man this is, even the winds and the waves obey Him. Matthew 8:23-27

When you are in a season where the storms are raging be reminded of this story, you are experiencing the wind and waves, but Jesus is right there with you guiding you through it.

I would be remiss not to speak about once you have weathered the storm and now you are on the other side. You must celebrate every victory after the storm has passed. A new season is on the horizon, get ready, it is a time and season for everything under the sun.

What is the moral of the story?

None of us know what we will face around the corner or what we may do while in the storm. However, Jehovah is the key to having peace in the midst of the storm, even if we do things to get out of the storm that may not be pleasing to God.

He is still a merciful and loving God, even when we try to take matters into our own hands.

He already knows our human frailties in the flesh.

What season are you currently experiencing?

Write it down, and journal when it started, and chronicle step by step so you can see where Jehovah is taking you in and through the process.

Prayer and reading the Word of God will help you pace yourself as you go through your season and time.

Some will say *I cannot even pray with what I am facing or going through.* But that is the time you ought to pray and ask the Holy Spirit what to pray for.

Many of us will ask to have the season quickly go or an answer to the difficult time and season we are in.

Usually, there will be no quick fix or answer given. In fact, the more you pray, the more challenging the season may become.

Then the question becomes "Why?"

Well, everyone's season is different, so the "why" question will be different for all of us.

There may be a lesson or teachable moment in your season.

Your course or direction may need to change in your life.

You may have lost someone very dear to you and are questioning God, "Why?"

Say, you are in preparation for what and where Jehovah wants to take you, and/or use you for His glory in the season.

Testimony may be what comes out of your season on how you were able to get through a challenging time and season and how He brought you through it.

CONSIDER THIS:

Our faith is constantly tested whether we equate this to a season or not.

Seasons will come and go, but where will you stand in your faith.

Jesus had to admonish His disciples when He said, "Oh you of little faith."

It is a question we all should ask ourselves daily, "Where do I stand in my faith?"

Your faith will be tested no matter what the season, in good or in challenging times.

When we do not see things changing in a season for the better, our faith may begin to waiver. It is here that we must be reminded of verse 1 in Hebrews 11: Faith is the substance of things hoped for, the evidence of things not seen.

Think about it, you just finished getting the car washed then the clouds form and it starts raining. Your first thought is I did not have to waste my time or money to wash the car if I knew it was going to rain.

Faith is like that; you will not know the details or the forecast, so you must trust Jehovah to lead and guide you.

If you take His hand, even with a blindfold, and He tells you to follow Him, you will not need to ask where you are going or what route is being taken. Let your blind faith hold His hand while he guides you.

It will require your patience because sometimes the journey may seem long and scary, but keep all your blind faith and trust Jehovah in and out of your seasons.

SIT AND LISTEN:

Never put a timeframe on your season(s). Remember the definition of *time*. If faith represents things not seen, let the challenge be that you trust in the mystery.

REFLECTIONS AND NOTES

As you reflect on this chapter, think about the season you are currently in and start journaling your journey. Do a faith check on yourself to determine where you are in your faith walk? Identify those areas that may be causing some doubt and fear to creep into your spirit and write them down and affirm daily the opposite. (e.g., Fear- Faith, Anger-Peace)

ROOM TO JOURNAL

_____

_____

_____

_____

_____

_____

_____

_____

_____

_____

_____

_____

_____

CHAPTER TWENTY

"THE TRUE AND GOOD SHEPHERD"

John 10: 1-5- "Most assuredly, I say to you, he who does
not enter the sheepfold by the door, but climbs up some other
way, the same is a thief and a robber. But he who enters by
the door is the shepherd of the sheep. To him the doorkeeper
opens, and the sheep hear his voice; and he calls his own sheep
by nae and leads them out. And when he brings out his own
sheep, he goes before them; and the sheep follow him, or
they know his voice. Yet they will by no means follow a
stranger, but will flee from him, for they do not know
the voice of strangers."

John 10 tells us that Jesus was a true and good shepherd because as He walked this earth, He patiently continued to impart wisdom about who His Father was and the relationship He had with His Father. Although others did not receive Him and questioned His teaching, He did not stop the journey. He knew what His Father sent Him to do and listened to the voice of His

Father. He knew what His purpose was while He was allowed to be in the physical flesh.

The scriptures often refer to Jesus as the "True Shepherd" to remind us that He was not an imposter. However, the more He showed who He was on His journey, the more people doubted Him. Many people witnessed the many miracles He performed, saw His compassion for others, and His love for those who were outcast by others. And yet, they still doubted who He was.

Isn't it frustrating when it seems you must prove yourself? You speak the truth, have a good heart, and others still question your motives or intentions. This the irony of being faithful. Because Jesus experienced ridicule and persecution while on earth, he can relate to what we go through as faithful followers of Him.

Because of what Jesus went through, we can follow Him and know that He understands what our life will be like. He's not calling us to do anything that he didn't do. It is an awesome feeling to have a Shepherd who will lead us and guide us. He brings us out of uncomfortable situations, and He goes in front of us. He will not allow us to be distracted by strange voices. When we allow the Holy Spirit to speak, the Father's voice is distinct to our ears. So, when we speak out what we hear. He backs us up and the naysayers must go somewhere and sit down.

Never deny Jesus. When He speaks, listen. He is our Shepherd and He speaks only truth. He is a good Shepherd and He proved Himself by sacrificing His life. The least we can do as His sheep is to bring others to the fold to hear His voice. Ask yourself, when was the last time you encouraged someone to meet the True and Good Shepherd?

CONSIDER THIS ANALOGY:

The Shepherd knows His sheep, and His sheep knows His voice.

When someone speaks out of their mouth, the tongue works in sync with the vocal cords and causes them to tremble and make the voice audible, so we hear the spoken word. Then your ear can receive and hear what is being spoken. The thing that you must know is that the Holy Spirit is sharing is the word through Sound.

Listen carefully, because as we hear these sounds, the Holy Spirit might be sending you a direct message. What sound is coming out of your mouth and entering your ears?

What is sound? It is vibrations that travel through the air-waves or another medium and can be heard when it reaches a person or an animal's ear.

The distinctive "voice "of Jehovah is like a vibration that only your ears can distinguish from any other voice and this vibration of continuous and regular vibrations should not be confused with noise.

The Holy Spirit should and will become a familiar voice to your ear. You will understand the language and the voice, and all other noises will be muted.

Have you ever spoken to someone on the telephone in a call you were not expecting, and you say your voice sounds familiar You wonder if we've spoken before on the phone? Or who is this?

Think of the telephone when it was first made available to the public. It was a party line. After a while it became what we call the main line. Now imagine your ear listening on either line.

Interference, distractions, interruptions, and multiple sounds amount to noise on the airwaves. All these noisy distractions will be found on the party line.

Jehovah's voice has a distinct sound and should be a familiar voice to our ears on the main line. It is better to stay on a line, which is crystal clear that does not have a bunch of subscribers, may offer noise, offers no privacy, and really allows any of us to pick up and listen.

Which line do you choose?

What do you want to hear?

Is the sound mumbled, or is the sound crystal clear?

SIT AND LISTEN:

1. What are you going to do when He speaks in your ear?

2. Will you be obedient and follow the instructions to a tee? Or will you ignore what you have heard?

3. Are you ready to receive the message and instructions? Sometimes just listening to the silence allows us to hear Jehovah's voice crystal clear.

REFLECTIONS AND NOTES

Take this time to answer the questions in this chapter and in the SIT AND LISTEN section and think of a moment when something was said to you, or you heard the voice of GOD and you had to decide if you were going to take heed and follow the instructions. Or question what you heard.

ROOM TO JOURNAL

_____

_____

_____

_____

_____

_____

_____

_____

_____

_____

_____

_____

_____

_____

CHAPTER TWENTY-ONE

"PRAYER IS A LIFESTYLE"

*Psalm 5: 1-3- Give ear to my words, O Lord, Consider
my meditation. Give heed to the voice of my cry, My King
and my God, For to You I pray. My voice You shall hear in
the morning, O Lord; In the morning I will direct it to You,
And I will look up.*

Often, when we pray, there is a specific reason or need. We are asking for help in a particular situation or guidance and direction on how we should move forward in deciding. Throughout the book of Psalms, David prays and asks for help and protection, for guidance, instructions, and directions in how to move forward. But he also showed us how to approach Jehovah when we pray.

Are you aware of how you approach Jehovah in your prayer time? How we come to Jehovah in prayer is just as important and more than the words we say.

Often, we come to God so focused on ourselves that we forget who He is. He is a pure and holy God. He deserves our respect. We should examine our-selves to see if we are approaching Him with

115

a clean and pure heart. He is our King, our Father and our Friend. We should make sure to give him a special time to pray. Sadly, we are all guilty of making prayer one of our last priorities when it should be our first. God is also all-knowing. He knows the answer to our request before we even ask, but we need to be willing to hear. Stop talking so much and let God talk to you. His words are so much more important than ours! Imagine, he is sitting there listening to you complain non-stop. He has the answer. He is just waiting for you to stop talking and listen to what He has to say.

The following steps are what I have used to transform my prayer life and my lifestyle in how I live for Jehovah.

STEP ONE: Come to Jehovah with humility and a spirit ready to spend quality time with Him. Humility is so important when approaching Jehovah. When we are humble we come to God as a little child to a parent. Void of ego, we look to him for guidance, kindness, compassion and truth. It is such a beautiful thing to approach Jehovah with humility. Don't become discouraged it may take time to develop this, but it is vital in strengthening our prayer time with Him. It may take time to develop this, but it is vital to strengthens our prayer time with Him.

STEP TWO: Ask for permission to enter His presence. Honor His holiness with praise and worship. Invite the Holy Spirit to fill you. Your prayer time should be led by the Holy Spirit, not your own thoughts.

STEP THREE: Sit with Him and allow His holy presence to speak to your heart. The Holy Spirit will unite both of your hearts as one. Acknowledge His presence and enjoy fellowship with Him. This is a time for bonding spiritually as He prepares to speak to you.

STEP FOUR: Communicate in the Holy Presence of Jehovah and ask for clarity in His wisdom and understanding. Now that you have humbly emptied yourself and allowed God's Spirit to lead you. You are now ready to communicate and her what Jehovah has to say to you.

What I share is my approach to spending time with Jehovah. Everyone will have different experiences but the key to having prayer time with Jehovah, is to come humbly and boldly. Yes, you can be bold in humility. But humility is the key to listening and hearing. Remember, any relationship worth having, you will have to work at it. If you put in the time and work, the relationship will flourish. If you do not spend time putting in the work, the relationship will suffer and then become disconnected. Put in the time with Jehovah, so the relationship will flourish and will stay connected.

Prayer is having a relationship with Jehovah. Spend time with Jehovah, and together your prayer life will unfold in ways you could never imagine.

CONSIDER THIS:

Praying for others is a good place to start on the road to your personal prayer time and relationship with Jehovah. If in your prayer time, Jehovah specifically asks that you pray for someone you have had an issue with, will you be obedient to Jehovah's instructions or will you ignore the instructions? Praying for others can set you up for blessings and put you on a path you could have never imagined because you put someone else's needs first. Jesus prayed for others and as expressed in John : 13, "Greater love hath no man to lay down His life for others." We all want our prayers answered, but are you willing to put your needs on the back burner and bring forth the needs of someone else?

SIT AND LISTEN:

Prayer is a lifestyle that we all should choose to adopt. The keyword is "choose."

A lifestyle guided by prayer is a lifestyle choice.

Sitting quietly to hear His voice in prayer and listening to His voice is a totally different thing.

ROOM TO JOURNAL

CHAPTER TWENTY-TWO

"WHO IS REIGNING IN YOUR LIFE?"

"The Lord Reigned: let the Earth rejoice; let the multitudes of isles be glad thereof. Clouds and darkness surround Him: righteousness and justice are the habitation of His throne. A fire goes before Him, and burneth up His enemies round about. His light is the light of the world; the earth saw and trembled. The hills melt like wax at the presence of the Lord, at the presence of the Lord of the whole earth. The heavens declare His righteousness and all the people see His glory." Psalm 97:1-6

The two words that dwell in my spirit are "reign" and "foundation." The definition of "reign" in Hebrew means, "May God reign." It also means to hold a royal office, as to rule as a king or queen. Jehovah holds the royal office. He is the Mighty King who will reign forever on His throne and Jesus is His son. God reigns over everything in the world and from underneath we need to let him reign over our lives. When he reigns in our lives with His attributes of forgiveness, repentance, regeneration and salvation we then have the foundation to live for God.

A foundation is a stone or concrete structure that supports a building with stability. When God reigns in our lives we have that foundation which gives the support and stability in our lives no matter what we may come up against.

When a king reigns over a country, the people in the land represent who he is. A ruthless, cruel king will be represented by a land that fears him, mistrusts, and follows in his cruel ways. However, a king that is kind and just will see the opposite. His people will follow his lead. They will be kind, just, helpful, and have an admiration for their king. The same is true of God. When we truly let Him reign in our lives, we will represent who He is. We will forgive because our God forgave us. We will share salvation with those around us because our God shared salvation with us. Our words and actions will represent Jehovah who reigns over us.

So, when you see this word, "reign" you should think of these words, forgiveness, repentance, regeneration, and salvation. Ask yourself daily, *Does my life represent these attributes of God? Do my actions show that he reigns over my life?*

Are you allowing Him to reign in your life, no matter what you face in this world? He reminds us He is a Sovereign and loving God, He will be exalted above all other gods, because He is King.

Compare your journey and work to have a firm foundation. When talking about a physical building, we are speaking in the context of building so it is structurally sound. The foundation is the lowest load-bearing part of a building, typically below ground level.

Is your foundation solidly in the ground? Will your spiritual house stand during normal acts of God? When there is a shaking of the ground, like an earthquake, will your house stand?

In Psalm 97, David reminds us of who is God and that He reigns over the earth and He preserves the souls of the saints. He delivers them out of the land of the wicked. Light is sown for the righteous, and gladness for the upright in heart. Isn't it a wonderful and awesome feeling? When we submit to the reign of Jehovah, he keeps us safe from the wicked forces that come against us.

CONSIDER THIS:

1. Who oversees your life?

2. Don't answer so quickly. I think most will say either they are or depending on or where they are in their journey, it could be a mate, parent, grandparents or caregiver. Think about it.

3. Are you satisfied with who you have put in charge or was it thrust on you with no say so in the decision making who is in charge?

4. If you want to make a change in your life, who would you put in charge?

5. Usually, you would or should want someone who will have your best interests at heart. You want a person who will consider your thoughts and discuss all the ramifications of any action. To be discussed could be making decisions on financial and investment opportunities, choosing a mate, what school

should the children attend, or what neighborhood should I purchase a home?

6. So then, ask yourself the question, "Who do you want to take charge?" Now do you see where we are going? There is only one reliable and logical person who can take charge, not be in charge. What is the difference you ask: When someone takes charge, there is no need to ask any questions. They are well versed in every area and can make the best decision for everyone involved.

Not trying to call anybody out, but if the shoe fits, put it on and walk in the truth.

6B. Can you speak the truth and be honest with yourself and Jehovah as to who you have allowed to be in charge, or are you opposed to giving up the reins to the King of kings and the Lord of lords?

At times, I have stepped back and let Him lead me, only to take charge when I felt He was taking too long. I would jump in front of him and find myself struggling to swim in the mess I made. If not for his grace and mercy, I may still be in some of those messes.

REFLECTIONS AND NOTES

I hope you took the time to answer the questions presented in the chapter. It is the starting point to getting the right things in place and allowing the take-charge King to take over.

Are you ready to make the necessary changes so HE can step in?

ROOM TO JOURNAL

_____

_____

_____

_____

_____

_____

_____

_____

_____

_____

_____

_____

_____

_____

CHAPTER TWENTY-THREE

"HE ALWAYS KEEPS HIS PROMISE"

Trust in the lord, and do good, Dwell in the land, and feed on His faithfulness. Delight yourself also in the Lord, And He shall give you the desires of your heart. Commit your way to the Lord, trust also in Him, And He shall bring it to pass. He shall bring forth your righteousness as the light, And your justice as the noonday. Psalms 37: 3-6

It is important to know the desires of your heart should be in unison with Jehovah's desires for your life. This may be a difficult concept to grasp, but if you are spending quality time with your Father, both your desires and His desires for your life will be in sync.

For many the problem is we do not put our trust in or stand on God's word. We, therefore, must learn to commit ourselves entirely to God and trusting only in him. This seems easy, until we are presented with difficult or trying times. I can attest to this in many situations/circumstances I have found myself in. The more my faith and patience was put to the test, the closer I came to the victory. I had to learn to trust God and not do my own thing. Scriptures remind us "to be anxious for nothing, but in prayer and supplication let your request be known" (Philip. 4:6).

Remember, when you are tired, frustrated, and anxious, God is still working. Jehovah reminds us, no matter what it looks like, what you see, hear, or encounter I keep my promises, my word will not come back void. You are closer to victory than you think. Whatever He has promised, if you believe and do not faint and grow weary it's coming. Commit yourself to endure until the end.

CONSIDER THIS:

We all have heard different sayings:

"Are you a man/woman of your word "

"Mean what you say, and say what you mean?"

In my high school yearbook, I wrote this as my life mantra. "Mean what you say and say what you mean." That was over forty years ago and I probably didn't fully grasp the depth of this phrase. Honestly, I cannot say I accomplish this every day, but I truly strive to live by this daily.

Jehovah knows our heart before we speak. *The word says, "for out of the abundance of the heart the mouth speaks." Matthew 12: 34*

So, do not be foolish in making such a vow/promise you do not intend to keep. If you make a vow to Jehovah, do not delay in keeping it. Meaning do not let your mouth open and must pay a bill, (make a promise) your pocketbook or wallet cannot afford.

SIT AND LISTEN:

In this quiet time, Jehovah said share three scriptures that fell on my heart inspired by the Holy Spirit:

"Oh Israel what does the Lord God require of you, but to fear the Lord, your God; to walk in all His ways and to love Him, to serve the Lord your God with all your heart and all your soul. And to keep the Commandments of the Lord and His statues, which I command you today for your good"

(Second tablets- Ten Commandments—the promise/Covenant of God to the people of Israel – Duet. 10:12).

Joshua 9:15 says, "So Joshua made a promise with them and made a covenant with them to let them live".

(Made a promise/ Covenant with those who had deceived Him) but He honored the Covenant.)

Herod kept a promise (oath) to the daughter of Herodias. She asked that John the Baptist's head be brought to her on a platter). Note: Her mother pushed her up to ask this of King Herod, after the daughter danced for Him at His birthday celebration. This is covered in Matthew 14:7-9

All three scriptures reference a promise that was made, and the consequences of those promises.

The moral of these stories is:

Never let anyone put you on the spot to do anything that you have not consulted with Jehovah about even if you made a promise.

REFLECTION AND NOTES:

1. What has been packed in your suitcase of promises?

2. Start with unpacking all the broken promises not kept and how it has impacted your life and others. Then forgiveness must be the key to the healing process to all involved.

ROOM TO JOURNAL

_____

_____

_____

_____

_____

_____

_____

_____

_____

_____

_____

_____

_____

_____

CHAPTER TWENTY-FOUR

"WHAT WE NOW SEE"

John 9: 1-5-Now as Jesus passed by, He saw a man who was blind from birth. And His disciples asked Him, saying "Rabbi, who sinned, this man or his parents, that he was born blind? Jesus answered " Neither this man nor his parents sinned, but that the works of God should be revealed in him. I must work the works of Him who sent Me while it is day; the night is coming when no one can work. As long as I am in the world, I am the light of the world."

As we draw closer to the final chapters, I hope you have come to an awakening and have a clearer understanding of yourself and of God.

In John 9:1-8, we read the story of a man who was blind since his birth. Jesus was walking with His disciples and passed the blind man. As they passed him, the disciples asked Jesus an odd question.

"Master who did sin, this man or his parents, that he was born blind?"

Jesus answered and told them.

"Neither this man sinned nor his parents: sinned but the works of God should be manifest in him. I must work the works of him who sent me while it is day: the night cometh when no man can work. As long as I am in the world, I am the light of the world."

As He had said these words, He spat on the ground and made clay with his saliva. Anointing the blind man with clay, Jesus instructed the man to go wash himself in the pool of Siloam. Following Jesus' instructions, the man returned and received his sight.

Just as this man was healed by following God's instruction, we can be healed as well. It is important to understand that not all healing is physical. Jesus heals spiritually and emotionally as well.

When he referred to himself as the light of the world that was symbolic of who He was. As long as people open their eyes to see Jesus, they will be able to see and not be blinded by the things of the world. Just like this man, many of us can remember and or relate when Jesus healed our spiritual eyes – allowing us to see Him for the first time in our lives.

There were some present that saw the miracle and had disbelief. They questioned if it really was the same man or some evil force was at play. Even following his explanation of what happened, they didn't believe.

Do you need to be awakened like the blind man? Would you trust Jesus if he gave you strange instructions? Would you believe a miracle if you saw one? Or, would you be like those that were blinded with disbelief? If we trust Jesus and look for Him, we will find that He has been right in front of us the whole time.

CONSIDER THIS:

Psalm 119, and Matthew 7 give many references to what we see, and then make us wonder.

When the Holy Spirit took me to these scriptures, let me be clear we all can see, yes see all the wrong in everybody else but ourselves. Jesus reminds us to not be judgmental, because we will be judged. How you measure others is how you will be measured.

Jesus asked,

"Why do you look at the specs in your brother's eye, but do not consider the plank in your eye?" Matthew 7:3

For the first time, I caught two things that I missed and maybe you did too when reading this. If not, then you are on point. A "speck" or specimen is small and often can only be seen close or under a microscope. But a "plank" as in a plank of wood is a considerable size and can be seen from a distance.

Jesus also said to the Pharisees,

"So how can you even move the specimen from your brother's eye before removing your plank? Do not be a hypocrite now".

Look at your shortcomings first. Make sure you have removed anything that keeps you from seeing with clarity as Jesus has instructed. Do not be judgmental or judge others. I have already been through the exercises of repenting and looking at my own shortcomings and I raised my hand when I began to feel free.

SIT AND LISTEN:

A doctor can test your vision to determine whether you have 20/20 vision which is considered having perfect vision. It means that we can see with our eyes exactly how they are supposed to work. However, that only measures our physical eyes. More important, we need to check our spiritual vision. How well can we see the spiritual world and the things of God? It does not matter what we see with our physical eyes if we are blind in our spiritual eye.

God opens your spiritual eye by revealing hidden things to you either through prophetic visions or words that may be written or spoken. If you want to see, your heart must be open to the Holy Spirit of Jehovah to see beyond the naked eye.

REFLECTIONS AND NOTES:

1. What are you allowing your eyes to see?

2. Have you ever experienced where you thought you saw something and when you further look or investigate it is something totally different?

3. Why couldn't you see clearly? Were you blinded physically or spiritually?

ROOM TO JOURNAL

_____

_____

_____

_____

_____

_____

_____

_____

_____

_____

_____

_____

_____

CHAPTER TWENTY-FIVE

"You Might Be Entertaining Angels"

Genesis 19:1-2- Now the two angels came to Sodom in the evening, and Lot was sitting in the gate of Sodom. When Lot saw them, he rose to meet them, and bowed himself with his face toward the ground. And he said, " Here now, my lords, please turn in to your servant's house and spend the night, wash your feet; then you may rise early and go on your way."

Genesis 19: 1-11 Speaks about Angels and if we are entertaining Angels. Are you? Will you in the future? Will you know?

Genesis 19:1-11 recounts Lots encounter with angels. In this story, Lot is sitting at the gate of Sodom. He sees two men walking in the square and greets them. He immediately realizes they are angels and invites them to his home. They had been sent to destroy the city of Gomorrah.

He acknowledged them and invited them into his home to spend the night and wash their feet, that they might rise in the morning and go on their way. The angels declined Lot's first invitation to rest in his home and said they would spend the night in the open square. But Lot insisted that they stay with him. The angels finally agreed to stay in the house and Lot made a feast and baked unleavened bread and they ate.

While Lot and the two angels were in the house, all the people of Sodom, young and old surrounded the house. They called for Lot, asking where the men are who came to you tonight. Bring them out so we can know them carnally. Sodom had become a place where wickedness was considered the normal practice.

This would lead us to believe the people wanted to see these two new men in the flesh. But if they knew they were entertaining angels, would they have acted in such a manner?

Lot's willingness to protect the Angels from the crowd led to the Angels safety. Had he not entertained the strangers he would have lost the blessing of safety.

Isn't it awesome when Jehovah steps in by sending one or more of His angels to snatch you from danger, by shielding you and protecting you from things known and unknown? These angels were on assignment as *Guardian Angels*. Nice company to have in a fight.

Angels are assigned to all of us to protect us, shield us, and warn us of dangers. Have you ever got out of dangerous situations/circumstances like domestic abuse, drug addiction, bankruptcy, homelessness or an illness? When you did, wasn't it a good feeling to be free?

All we must do is call on them and they will be dispatched from Jehovah to us. The angels then asked Lot if he had anyone else in the city because they would give them time to leave before they destroyed Sodom and Gomorrah. We all feel we know how the story continues to unfold but it helps to study the scriptures. Lot gathered his family, and still lingered. Some of his family thought it was a joke, so the angels took Lot and his family's hands and put them outside of the city.

But here we find the most important words in the scripture. The angels told Lot to "Escape for your life, but do not look back."

When Jehovah sends a warning, we must take heed. We may not get all the details, but we must listen to the warning and follow the instructions to a tee. Remember we cannot see around the corner of life's journey or what is ahead.

Have you ever been delayed getting out of the house?

You cannot find your car keys or your wallet. Then you leave just five minutes later, and as you approach the red light two blocks away there is an accident. You think to yourself, five minutes sooner, I could have been involved in the accident. The delay may have irritated you or even frustrated you, but it was probably your saving grace and an angel who delayed you.

Say you missed your train, and another train comes, and the conductor advises there is a stalled train with mechanical difficulties in the tunnel. Then the conductor says *We will be going down the express track.* The train you are on by passes the stalled train, and you see all the people stuck. You can tell I live and have worked in a major city. It's New York in my case.

Sometimes our main source of getting to work or an interview is the reason that makes us late for work or that interview. Some things will not be under our control. The key is to always make sure you did your absolute best to leave early enough to be on time.

Not trying to sound creepy, but angels are defined as spiritual beings. Some believe them to act as an attendant or agent, a messenger of God, a guardian of humans, and far superior to humans in power.

We left off at the story that Lot was grateful that the angels had mercy and favored him and his family, saving their lives. It was good that he had already figured out that they would not die in the mountains, and the city of Zoar would be better. So, the angels guided them to the city of Zoar. With Lot and his family far away and safe, the Lord rained brimstone and fire on Sodom and Gomorrah. But again, we find the most important words in the scripture and I lay it out for you." Escape for your life, but do not look back." Lot's wife did look back. She was evaporated into salt.

CONSIDER THIS:

I cannot remember the day, month or year, but I do recall I felt defeated in my personal and professional life. I had just missed my train to work around 6:45 am. It was interesting that at 42nd Street, the platform was virtually empty.

I sat down, discouraged and I remember seeing this elderly Caucasian man walking toward me. The distinct thing about him was he had a beautiful smile – pearly white teeth–and blue/green eyes that appeared to change color. He was well groomed in a suit and hat with white hair and a low beard.

After he sat down, he began to talk. Yes, in New York, he began to speak to me. He said,

You have a beautiful smile, and you are a beautiful woman, and the best is yet to come. Surprised, I said thank you because

I really needed that. I turned my head briefly because I thought I heard the train coming and I got up as the train pulled into the station. I looked around and the man was nowhere to be found. He had vanished in thin air. I knew at that moment that it was an angel sent to encourage me and I often am reminded of that encounter when I need encouragement.

Will you know if you have entertained an angel? We have all have had close calls —a near car accident, a slip or fall, where we can only credit our safety to seeming chance or coincidence. Those instances weren't chance. They were angels sent from God to protect us. When you feel danger, call on your angels for help.

SIT AND LISTEN:

Sit in meditation and prayer time and ask Jehovah and the Holy Spirit to send you an Angel. Ask for insight, guidance, instructions, comfort, and peace. Since the Holy Spirit is activated when we are in oneness with Jehovah in a relationship the angel will come. Be patient.

REFLECTION AND NOTES:

1. Have you encountered an angel that has helped you out of a difficult situation?

2. Have you entertained an angel? Did you know?

ROOM TO JOURNAL

_____

_____

_____

_____

_____

_____

_____

_____

_____

_____

_____

_____

_____

_____

CHAPTER TWENTY-SIX

"WHAT MIRACLE ARE YOU BELIEVING FOR?"

Luke 5:18-20-Then behold. men brought on a bed a man who was paralyzed, whom they sought to bring in and lay before Him. Ad when they could not find how they might bring him in, because of the crowd, they went up on the housetop and let him down with his bed through the tiling into the midst before Jesus. When He saw their faith, He said to him, "Man, your sins are forgiven you."

When we hear the word *miracles*, most of us think of something occurring in the natural human experience, which is unexplainable. However, everyday miracles happen all around us seen and unseen. Those that we can see are of physical nature where through our eyes we are shown something that either can be explained or can't be explained. This can be where a healing has taken place through a medical procedure or a supernatural occurrence that can't be explained.

Healing is to make free from injury or disease; or to make sound or whole; or to make well again; and/or to restore to original purity or integrity.

In Luke 5:17, Jesus was teaching the Pharisees and teachers of the law sitting by, who had come out of every town of Galilee, Judea and Jerusalem. And the power of the Lord was present to heal them. While they were there, men brought a man who was paralyzed on a bed. As they attempted to bring Him before Jesus, the crowd was too great, so they went up to the roof of the house and lowered Him down into the house and laid Him before Jesus.

When Jesus saw what they went through to get the paralyzed man into the house, because if they could just get in the room with Jesus the man would be healed. Jesus recognized their faith and said, "Man your sins are forgiven you."

Forgiving the man's sins first is significant because at that moment he was healed spiritually which manifested into his physical healing.

Would you go through those great lengths to get into the room with Jehovah?

Would you go this length just to have an audience with Him?

Or would you give up the minute you saw a massive crowd?

He loves us so much that once we step in the room and our heart is opened to receive forgiveness the healing process is inevitable.

There were specific instructions in this miracle, Jesus told the man to take up his bed and go to your house. The paralyzed man who was now healed immediately did exactly what Jesus told him to do. He rose before them, took up what He had been lying on and departed to His house, glorifying God.

I think you get the gist of the story. Healing is tied in a knot to forgiveness and faith.

As we are in awe of what Jesus did, people who witnessed these healings and miracles still questioned His authenticity.

Obviously, people may question your authenticity, but you must stand firm in your beliefs and your faith.

In Luke 7, Jesus heals a centurion servant. Again, Jesus heals the servant because of his faith.

The servant did not even think he was worthy of Jesus coming to his house. But Jesus hearing of his faithfulness to other people made his house a house to which Jesus wanted to go. Jesus marveled and told the crowd, *"I say to you, I have not found such great faith, not even in Israel."* Now I say to you, do you have a house that Jesus wants to visit?

Hebrew 11:16- And without faith it is impossible to please God, because anyone who comes to him must believe that he exists and that he rewards those who earnestly seek him.

The centurion servant's faithfulness to Jehovah was rewarded and healed from his sickness.

CONSIDER THIS:

Sometimes we may think we are not worthy to come to Jehovah or be in His presence. We have sinned, been backsliders, and made other mistakes. Jesus still promises that he will come to our house to heal and forgive if we let him in. There are some perquisites that we must adhere to have this promise: Repent and ask forgiveness, forgive others, and put your faith and trust in Jehovah.

SIT AND LISTEN:

Faith is the key to believing that you can be healed and that miracles are possible with Jehovah at the helm. If you have breath in your body, there is always hope, no matter the situation or circumstance.

REFLECTION AND NOTES:

How many times have you questioned if we would come out from an illness or situation that looked dismal on the surface? We question GOD, as to why or what did we do to warrant this plight. We pray for healing, but it seems to be taking for ever to get a breakthrough. You, see or hear about others being healed or delivered and you find yourself still in a battle fighting for your life.

You pray and still no answer or direction given in how you should proceed. Have you thought this is something GOD is working through you so he can show his mighty hand through a miracle?

Never give up hope, your faith may be tested, your testimony will stand the test of time.

ROOM TO JOURNAL

_____

_____

_____

_____

_____

_____

_____

_____

_____

_____

_____

_____

_____

_____

CHAPTER TWENTY-SEVEN

"WHERE IS YOUR FAITH?"

Romans 10:17 "So then faith cometh by hearing and hearing by the word of God.

Where is your faith? Will you believe in what you cannot see? And trust what you hear?

God shared an acronym with me for how faith operates. This ACRONYM defines and gives life to each letter in the word faith. I invite you to add your own words as we travel through this list.

F – Fearless/Foundation
A – Advocate
I – Insight.
T – Truth/Trust
H – Humility

F – Fearless/Foundation: Let us start with being fearless by defining it. When one thinks of the word *fear*, we associate it with being afraid.

When we think of a foundation, we think about having something to hold something – us in this case. As the world battled COV-19 a virus that caused sickness and death, fear gripped the world.. Now is the time to be reminded of the scripture found in Deuteronomy 31:6. It says, "Be strong and of good courage, fear not, nor be afraid of them: for the Lord thy God, is the One who goes with you. He will not leave you nor forsake you." When we operate in faith, there is a foundation that God plants our feet on "solid ground." It allows us to be built-up where we are weak because we are rooted in God's Word. The earth may shake, and the winds may blow you in all kind of directions, but the solid *foundation* will keep you standing in faith.

A – **Advocate:** God is our advocate. God, Jesus, the Holy Spirit and the angels work together to advocate or fight for us. When someone *advocates* for you it is someone who has faith in your person or share a belief pertaining to an idea/concept. Biblically an "advocate" is referenced as the Holy Spirit either sent by God or something living inside of us. An *Advocate* will fight for us as our faith is strengthened in Jehovah.

I – **Insight:** Insight is defined as the ability or the capacity to gain an accurate and deep intuitive understanding of a person or thing. The biblical meaning speaks to having wisdom. When you breakdown this word, two words are derived from it: *"In"* and *"Sight."* When you are "in" something, you are a part of it. When you have "sight" You can envision it manifesting itself. He instructs us to share when you have *insight.* You see into the depths of one's heart and soul through the Holy Spirit. When our faith brings *"in"* and *"sight"* together there is a marriage in the Holy Spirit. This marriage allows us to see beyond what we maybe do not see through our faith.

T -**Trust:** The next letter on our faith journey is *Trust.* God's Word is *truth,* and it will stand the test of time. Matthew 24:35 tells us that heaven and earth shall pass away, but His word will never pass away. If we believe and stand on Jehovah's Word, then we must *trust* and have faith that what He said in the word is true. When someone is called to testify in court, they place their right hand on the Bible and are asked the question." Do you solemnly swear to tell the whole truth and nothing but the truth so help me God.

When you have your private time with Jehovah, will you be honest with Him and speak the truth? Will you trust that His word is true?

We must allow the Holy Spirit and our heart to *trust* that Jehovah will work out any and every situation for our good. Even when we cannot see the outcome.

You might as well speak the *truth* to him. *Trust* me He can see your heart anyway.

H- **Humility:** Humbleness to many is perceived as a sign of weakness. But to Jehovah true *humility* is one of the greatest things to have and He sees it as a sign of strength. The words *"Humble"* and *"Humility "* come from the same root word HUMILIS, which is Latin for 'low or close to the ground.' *Humble* is the adjective so it is used to describe someone, whereas *humility* is the noun. They both refer to someone who is not arrogant or proud. Proverbs 15:33 tells us that the fear of the Lord is instruction of wisdom, and before honor is *humility.*

Now we all have done and accomplished things that we are proud of—say completed our education and obtained a degree. You fill in the blank.

We receive accolades from our family and friends. We even will thank them for their support and encouragement while on the Journey. Do not get me wrong, it is a wonderful thing to celebrate one's accomplishments. Jehovah loves to see us do well and have great achievements.

But, you knew this was coming.

Do we forget or need to be reminded sometimes we would have not ever gotten to first base or even made the team without Him giving us the tools or talent.

We are only who we are because of (you) Jehovah and we acknowledge you. We will never forget that we are nothing without you. Man will fail us and make promises they cannot keep, but your promise will stand the test of time. We honor you and adore you.

Faith is in full operation when you humble yourself before Jehovah knowing in Him, we have nothing to fear. God and the Holy Spirit serve as your advocate and fill you with insight. As you are filled with insight you discover God's Truth, and you are filled with humility as you walk with God.

REFLECTIONS AND NOTES

1. Write out the things, situations or circumstances that have shaken and questioned your FAITH.

2. Affirm daily that these things, situations and circumstances can no longer have a stronghold over you. Remind yourself that your faith will be tested but you will stand on the promise of GOD in his Word.

ROOM TO JOURNAL

CHAPTER TWENTY-EIGHT

"WHO ARE YOU SERVING WITH YOUR TALENTS."

Romans 12:6- 8- Having then gifts differing according to the grace that is given to us, let us use them: if prophecy, let us prophesy in proportion to our faith; or ministry, let us use it in our ministering, he who teaches, in teaching, he who exhorts, in exhortation, he who gives, with liberality; he who leads, with diligence; he who shows mercy, with cheerfulness.

In Romans 12, the question deep in the reading really asks us, whom are you serving with your talents and gifts?

In the biblical sense talent and gifts are defined as:

> Talent: generally defined as a natural aptitude, ability or skill and often it is done naturally and with little effort. It is often and unfortunately associated with having money.

> Gift: is defined as a thing given willingly to someone without payment.

Jehovah has equipped each of us with specific talents and gifts to share with the world. Our contribution does not need to be as profound an invention or a major discovery. It can be as simple as checking on our sick and elderly neighbor, volunteering at a homeless shelter or food bank, being educated with a talent and memory to entertain others, a beautiful voice, etc. and other simple things we do with our time or enhance with education. Whatever our gift is, it is our duty to use it. The beauty of God's gifts or a talent is that it is bestowed upon you and you do not have to pay for either. They both are freely given and you get to maintain them if you allow the anointing of the Holy Spirit to nurture the gifts and/or talents by using them to share with others, where God will get all the glory.

ANOINTING

In Psalm 23:5, David writes that God 'anoints my head with oil.' This anointing of oil during that time represented the anointing of God's spirit. Anytime a leader was raised up in Israel, he was symbolically 'anointed' with oil. The same is true today. God gives us gifts and talents, and when we surrender to them for his glory, He bestowes upon us a special anointing.

A perfect example of this is where two singers sing beautifully and have naturally born talent. What is the difference? Both have the talent, but only one has the anointing.

Know that sometimes your efforts may seem to be unnoticed or unrecognized. It was over seven years after his anointing before David was crowned king. Allow the anointing of God to fill you, and in time, you will see that your gifts and efforts are making a difference.

Have you taken the time to sit and truly know what gift(s)/ talent(s) Jehovah has equipped you with? And the purpose and destiny it is to fulfill and accomplish while you live on this Earth. Explore this logically with the word and how Jehovah would. Do not look at it the way the world would. Scripture says He will make room for your gifts. If you still are unclear of what gifts and talents you have inside of you, spend some time with Jehovah in prayer, asking for the direction and the Holy Spirit to guide you.

MAKE ROOM FOR YOUR GIFT

Proverbs 18:16 tell us a man's gifts make room for him. God has put a gift or talent in every person. Not only does the world have room for your gift, but it's also waiting for you to fill the space reserved for it. It is the gift that will enable you to fulfill your vision. It will make a way for you in life. When God makes room for your gifts, He has carved out time and space for it to manifest itself at the appointed and appropriate time. The gift will come when it is ready. You do not want to get ahead of it, but you also don't want to lag when it arrives. Always have room for your gift, so you are ready when God presents it to you.

So, let us go to Romans 12:2-3, where we are reminded not to think more highly of ourselves. And be not conformed to this world: be ye transformed by the renewing of your mind, that ye may prove what is good, and acceptable, and perfect, will of God. Remember God's perfect "will" for us.

When we let our "mind" and our "will" get us caught up in how the world thinks we should share our gifts and talents we will never fulfill the true purpose of using our gifts and talents for Jehovah to get the glory.

Every gift and talent is for Him to show His glory and shine through us to share the gifts and talents.

As we come to a close on gifts and talents let us look at Romans 12:3,6-7

"For I say, through the grace given unto me, to every man that is among you not to think of himself more highly than He ought to think; but to think soberly, according as God hath dealt to every man the measure of faith." Having then gifts differing according to the grace that is given to us, whether prophecy, let us prophesy according to the proportion of faith."

So, if you trust Jehovah and have faith that He has made room for your gifts and talents, wait patiently and do the work in preparation so, when he brings you into the room to show you off to the world, they will know from where the gifts and talents come from-Jehovah. It goes on to share the different gifts: ministering, teaching, and how we should present ourselves when honoring God in our gifts and talents.

When we come forth, we are representing the King with these gifts and talents. He said to tell them ACT like it.

CONSIDER THIS:

A- Anointing will be all over the gifts and talents.
C – Christ-like spirit when you share and serve others using the gifts and talents.
T- Teach others through your gifts and talents.

Remember who you are serving with the GIFTS and TALENTS I gave you.

Your gift and talent is yours Alone.

Jehovah reminded me that everyone has something to offer as I gave them to share.

He doesn't want us to squander our gift(s) and talent(s).

To squander means to waste time in a wreckless and foolish manner or allow an opportunity to pass or be lost.

Please I beg of you, use your God Given talents: Share with others; to be a blessing to others; and a blessing to the body of Christ- His Kingdom

You have no TIME to WASTE

For the kingdom of God is at hand.

SIT AND LISTEN:
A Short Prayer:

Dear God,

Thank you that you have given me gifts and that you have made room for me to use these gifts. Let me align with your will in the use of my gifts and talents. I pray that I focus on you. Many may not understand or agree with the gift you have given me. Thank you for the race you have started me on. Help me get to the finish line.

REFLECTIONS AND NOTES

Write down your talents and gifts and start utilizing them to serve others.

ROOM TO JOURNAL

_____

_____

_____

_____

_____

_____

_____

_____

_____

_____

_____

_____

_____

_____

CHAPTER TWENTY-NINE

"UNCHARTED WATERS"

Matthew 8: 23-27- Now when He got into a boat, His disciples followed Him. And suddenly a great tempest arose on the sea, so that the boat was covered with the waves. But He was asleep. Then His disciples came to Him and awoke Him, saying, "Lord, save us! We are perishing!" But He said to them, "Why are you fearful, O you of little faith?" Then He arose and rebuked the winds and the sea, and there was a great calm. So the men marveled saying, "who can this be, that even the winds and the sea obey Him?"

Uncharted waters are defined *as a situation or circumstances that is foreign or unfamiliar, or unclear, and which may be dangerous or difficult territory because it is not on a map.*

Matthew 8 shares a story where the disciples were afraid during a storm. One could say they found themselves in uncharted waters. It reads as follows:

"And when He was entered into a ship, His disciples followed Him. And behold, there arose a great tempest in the sea, in so much that the ship was covered with the waves: but He was asleep. And His disciples came to Him and awoke Him, saying, "Lord save us: we perish. And He saith unto them, "why are you fearful, O ye of little faith?" Then He arose and rebuked the winds and sea, and there was a great calm. But the men marveled, saying, what manner of man is this, that even the winds and the sea obey Him!?"

Jesus reminded the disciples that although they were afraid during a storm and these uncharted waters, but He was right there with them. They all had been witness to many of His Miracles and saw how His spirit was compassionate and could bring peace. Why doubt Him now? When we get into storms and in unfamiliar waters, we will be fearful because of the unknown situations or circumstances that may happen. In this moment, will fear take over or will your faith in God give you peace?

We all have been in "Uncharted" waters. We have encountered storms where we feel that we are overwhelmed by the raging sea of life. We do not know if the "ship" (your body) will hold up in the storm. Our spirit is weak, and we are crippled by the fear within us. and our spirit is weak or seemingly have no strength when fear grips us.

The problem is that when faced with these situations, we often forget to turn to Jehovah for help. Many times, I have found myself in the middle of the storm and I have tried to fix it myself. Every time I do this, without fail, I make the storm worse. The disciples were right next to Jesus and were fearful. They forgot who they were with! We must have faith in He who guides our boat. Remember Jesus said to His disciples, "O ye of little Faith."

I learned this the hard way. I did my own inner searching and realized that most of the time, when I was in uncharted waters; I would try to figure a solution out without asking for help from Jehovah. After I realized this and strengthened my faith in him, I began to see Him work in the storms. The uncharted waters became calm, and I found peace in Jehovah.

Remember the acronym for faith?

1) Being Fearless,
2) Knowing we have an Advocate in the Holy Spirit,
3) Letting our spiritual eye let us have Insight,
4) Trusting Him,
5) Staying Humble

CONSIDER THIS:

A river is a large natural stream of water flowing in a channel to the sea, lake or another such stream. We all should want "Peace" like a river, but what does it truly mean? It means that despite the ebb and flow of circumstances, peace washes over you like a river.

Peace reassures you that you are safe in the middle of everything. When we allow the natural flow of our river the Holy Spirit brings us our peace and will keep us calm in all situations and circumstances no matter the danger we may encounter.

When we flow in the Holy Spirit, we are allowing the flowing of living waters of peace to wash and cleanse us. Remember we are a spirit living in a body covered in flesh. If our inner spirit is at peace, then our outer body will reflect that peace on the outside.

You must decide if you want peace that flows like a river, irrespective of what is going on, what you see or what you hear. (You fill in the blank).

"Now the God of hope fill you with all joy and peace in believing, so that you may abound in hope, through the power of the Holy Ghost." Romans 15:13

SIT AND LISTEN: REFLECTION AND NOTES

1. Have you ever been sitting on the beach and the water is tranquil and serene and suddenly you see the clouds forming and the ocean becomes angry, and a storm comes out of nowhere?

2. What do you do? How do you handle the "uncharted" waters?

3. Take note of a time you encountered such a time in your life and recall how you got through it.

ROOM TO JOURNAL

CHAPTER THIRTY

"WHAT IS YOUR MOUNTAIN?"

We often compare life to climbing a mountain. As we pursue our goals and purpose in life, we find that it can be an uphill battle. This uphill journey is made easier when we follow God. He doesn't always remove the mountain, but he may just provide a staircase. Each step we take in our life's journey will require us to move forward and step up to new challenges and obstacles. Just like a staircase, we must move up one step at a time, and sometimes, to move on to the next chapter, we must also be ready to step down as well.

Let us talk about stepping forward and stepping up. There are stairs to climb so I now ask, "What is your Mountain?"

Pulling definitions out of the workings of a staircase we find:

A *staircase* is a fixed helix of ascending stationary blocks that help us climb a height in a building or house. Usually, a secure railing is fixed on the wall or on vertical poles at the side for which you can hold on.

As we move through our journey we will encounter stair steps where we will have to access each step in the process to determine if we are moving in God's will for our lives or have a mis-step and needed to reassess where we are in the process.

Each component of the *staircase* is important to the structure and the foundation of the stairs are sturdy enough to help support our stepping from one step to get to the next step as we climb to our next level.

So, when we step forward on our journey in life we are saying I am ready for the next assignment or opportunity that has been presented by Jehovah. Especially if we find ourselves going around a landing separated by a wall.

The word "forward" means to go in the direction you are facing or traveling; toward the front or onward as to make progress; toward a successful conclusion.

MOSES AND HIS STEPS

The spirit now brings me back to Moses. From before his birth, Moses was chosen by God to save the Israelites from Egypt. God orchestrated every *step* of Moses' life to prepare him for his destination. Most of us know the story of Moses, but today, we will detail how God led Him step by step. He had to climb each step one at a time; he could not skip or jump over any of the steps. By following each step God gave him, he was able to lead an entire nation out of slavery.

BOTTOM OF THE STAIRCASE

We all know Moses was the Hebrew infant and the miracle that floated down the Nile River into the hands of the barren daughter of the Pharaoh who was to raise him after his birth mother had to get him out of a troubled house. When he was grown, having learned he was Hebrew he yearned to be among his people.

So, let us start with Exodus 2. Moses saved a Hebrew slave by accidently killing an Egyptian who was flogging him. But as it is in many instances, the Hebrew slave did not appreciate it thinking Moses was an Egyptian prince and not one of them. But once Moses realized what he had done was known by some of the Hebrew slaves, he feared that Pharaoh would hear of him killing an Egyptian and would set out to kill him.

THE MIDDLE OF THE STAIRCASE.

Moses fled to Midian were Hemet the daughters of the Priest of Midian who was a Reuel – meaning a friend of God.

While the daughters were drawing water the shepherds drove the daughters from the well, but Moses protected them and then assisted the daughters while tending to the flock. Upon their return home they shared with their father that an Egyptian, who delivered them from the shepherds, had then helped them to tend the flock. So, their father inquired, "*Why did you leave Him?*"

They sent for Moses so He could eat bread with them. Moses lived with the Priest and He was given His daughter Zipporah and she bore a son Gershom. As time passed Moses heard that the King of Egypt died. The children of Israel continued to cry out to God, and He heard their cries. God remembered His covenant with Abraham, Isaac and Jacob and acknowledged the children of Israel. Moses was getting ready to go to levels he could only achieve by stepping up and being obedient to Jehovah.

(Exodus 3) starts to unfold as to how God presented himself to Moses and gave him the steps and instructions he was to take as he prepared to go back to Egypt to deliver His people. Remember Moses was born to Hebrew parents. So, God had chosen Him for this specific assignment while in His mother's womb.

Moses was visited by an Angel of the Lord in a flame of fire in a bush, and when He went to turn and look to see this bush that did not burn, he heard the voice of God from the midst of the bush, saying Moses,

"Here I Am. Draw not nigh hither. Take your shoes off your feet whereon thou stand is holy ground. I am the God of your Father, God of Abraham, God of Isaac and of Jacob."

Moses is afraid as he hears from God. But God had seen the oppression of the children of Israel, and it was now the "ripe time" to free them. God advises Moses He is sending Him to Egypt to tell Pharaoh "To Let My People Go".

Can you imagine, you hear from Jehovah and He tells you He is sending you on a mission exclusively to free someone and you know the challenges before you?

You would think it was a mission impossible. Most of us remember the show "Mission Impossible", where the team was given a mission that was virtually impossible. Instructions were given then the tape of instructions imploded.

When Jehovah gives us a mission, it can be scary because of the unknown, but He never leaves us alone. Every step is mapped out, and all we must do is follow the instructions step by step. Scripture says, with God all things are possible (Matthew 19:26) We then carry the tape of instructions in our heart.

Moses asked Jehovah in (Exodus 3:11) "Who am I that I should go to Pharaoh and I should bring forth the children of Israel out of Egypt?"

Jehovah said, "*Certainly I will be with thee: and this shall be a token unto thee, that I have sent thee: When you have brought forth the people out of Egypt ye shall serve God on this mountain.*"

Moses continued his important dialogue with God by asking 'Who do I say sent me?'

God responded by telling Moses to reply, '*The God of your fathers has sent me*' they then will say to you 'What is His name?' and you are to answer 'I AM THAT I AM.'

And to the children of Israel, you will say 'I AM has sent me to you.'

God then gives Moses his next step to climb in the process. Moses was instructed to gather all the Elders and advise them that, 'The Lord God of your fathers, the God of Abraham, of Isaac, and of Jacob, appeared to me saying,

"I have surely visited you and seen what is done to you in Egypt and I will bring you up out of your affliction of Egypt to the land of the Canaanites and the Hittites and the Amorites and the Perizzites and the Hivites and the Jebusites, to a land flowing with milk and honey.' Exodus 3:16-17.

God assures Moses that the Israelites would heed your voice and come to you.

These were hard instructions, but God was not finished. Each step in the process on the staircase would become more challenging as He ascended.

God showed Moses through signs and wonders or miracles that he would be equipped to go before Pharaoh. God showed His power by turning the rod and staff that Moses carried into a serpent. God showed His power when the leprous hand that when placed in His bosom and removed was restored. God showed His power when he turned water into blood.

Jehovah knew Pharaoh was not going to adhere to the signs, but we should look at His strengthening the face of Moses, while repeatedly giving Pharaoh a chance to soften his heart.

It is overlooked in most biblical depictions, but I think it is important to note that Moses was concerned He would not be able to do the assignment because He had a speech impediment. This is a good reminder to us all. When God chooses you, He will always give you the necessary tools and skills to complete the assignment – even if you feel that you are not prepared. God said to Moses,

"Who has made man's mouth? Who makes the mute, the deaf, the seeing or the blind? Have not I? Therefore, go and I will be with your mouth and teach you what you have been instructed to say." (reference?) Exodus 4:11

Moses still doubted He was capable or able. This angered God, but He still showed mercy to Moses and assigned Aaron the Levite and Moses' brother to be his advocate.

"I know He can speak well, and is coming to meet you, and when He sees you, He will be glad in His heart."

God instructed Moses to speak to his brother Aaron, informing him he had been chosen to be the mouth piece to speak on behalf of Moses, as God gives instructions.

FINAL STEPS

God had given Moses everything he would need to complete the mission. This was the final step in the staircase. Leading the children of Israel out of Egypt into the promise land. Many obstacles presented itself on the journey, Moses had to contend with the complaining of the people and questioned God as to why he would bring them out and have them wondering around in the wilderness.

Those final steps to the top often are the most difficult to endure as you may become tired and weary.

THE MOUNTAIN TOP

Although it took forty years for the children of Israel to reach the promise land, Moses stood on the mountain top and saw the promise land and then his journey was complete. He went through many things to reach the mountain top. There is a litany of events and instructions in the book of Exodus given to Moses as he ascended the stairs to the mountain top.

1) *Moses was instructed to carry the rod and staff to do signs.*

2) *God sent Aaron into the wilderness to meet Moses so that Moses could share with him all that God had said. The two of them were advocates in their faith.*

3) *Let us not forget that Moses had a very devoted wife to help him.*

4) *There was famine and locusts upon the Egyptians.*

5) *The death of the firstborn affected Pharaoh directly*

6) *The Israelites crossed the Red Sea.*

7) *Bread rained down from Heaven.*

8) *But the ungratefulness, disbelief and honor of false gods left the Israelites to spend over 40 years in the desert.*

9) *Moses was not able to enter the Promise Land for his disobedience to GOD when he was told to speak to the rock to bring forth water. Instead, he struck the rock.*

Is not Jehovah amazing how He prepares us for the journey, He has the appointed time and place, but we must be obedient. Every step in the journey prepared Moses for the next step up until reaching the Mountain top.

CONSIDER THIS:

1. A song that I Live by is "Order My Steps" by Glenn E. Burleigh. What song or movie encourages you in your climb?

2. What stairs have you had to climb? Or has it been a mountain?

1. What other circumstances and/or instructions do you find in Exodus?

REFLECTION AND NOTES:

1. What was a specific time in your Journey when the mountain seemed too hard to climb but you continued?

2. How did you grow stronger and better during this time?

3. Remind yourself of the steps you took to get there.

4. Reflect on how God was with you and helped you during that time.

ROOM TO JOURNAL

_____

_____

_____

_____

_____

_____

_____

_____

_____

_____

_____

_____

_____

CHAPTER THIRTY-ONE

"SOME RAIN MUST FALL"

Rain must fall, and the sun must shine. What is their purpose? Often, we are appreciative of the sunlight, but less enthusiastic about rainfall. Sunlight makes us happy, helps trees to grow, and makes for a great beach day. It's easy to see why we like the sun. However, though less appreciated by many, rain is as equally important as the sun.

THE POWER OF RAIN AND THE SUN

Rain is a necessary element of life. It cleanses the earth and atmosphere of impurities, it gives life to trees, and provides drinking water for creatures and humans alike. Simultaneously, it washes your body and exhilarates the mind as you run through a storm. It ends a heat wave and quells a drought. However, the same rainfall can raise humidity to unbearable levels. It can overflow rivers, flood streets, and cause severe damage to property. Rain can be both a blessing and a curse.

The Sun is defined as a star around which the Earth orbits. The sun shines on the earth bringing warmth and other life-giving properties. We often long for the feel of the warm sun on our face. We take trips to beaches, we sunbathe, and plan summer activities to be in the warmth of the sun. However, just like the rain, the sun can also be damaging. Without the balance of rain, the sun can scorch the earth and cause a drought. The sun can cause a heat stroke or death if we are under its rays too much.

In our journey of life, rain will fall, and the sun will shine. We all want blessings to shine down on us, on our family, and love ones. No one wants suffering to befall them, or see anyone they love/care about suffer from the challenges of life.. The truth is we need both. Our life is completed when we embrace the power of the rain and of the sun. However, Jehovah did not promise that difficult days won't come. He gave us the promise and hope that when we trust in Him, He will bring us through every storm. So, whether under the rays of the sun or the drops of rain, we learn to be content and embrace the power of both.

GOD SPEAKS THROUGH THE RAIN.

It is hard to ignore the destructive nature of rain. It makes sense that a good rain is necessary for life and for cleansing the air, but why is rain also destructive? Why would a loving God allow such a thing? Because He cares. God allows blessings to rain down on all of us, but sometimes we don't listen. Sometimes we take His blessings for granted and forget Him. When it rains and storms come, we are forced to take notice. These storms serve as a wakeup call, a call for justice. The earth is being washed and purged both physically and spiritually. The rain could be viewed as God's tears as He calls us to follow Him.

Our job is to recognize His call and respond. We have the ability to change the world and share God through our actions. We should love when others hate. Show compassion when others are angry. Give when others are selfish. Share openly when others discriminate. Through these actions, we can bless others. We can bring a gentle cleansing rain or share a warm ray of hope. If we all start practicing just one of these, we could show Jesus to the world.

CONSIDER THIS:

Remember, there is a purpose to everything that happens in our world.

The rain must fall, and the sun must shine.

What is your purpose during these "acts of God?" Your purpose becomes the question.

Why do you exist now, and during these times and in this space and time?

Can you say with clarity you know your purpose on this Earth?

Are you here to change something, effect a change, or do you need to change to bring about a change?

We all will experience rainstorms and sunshine in our lives. How we are able to withstand it depends on our relationship with Jehovah. He is the Master Teacher, and He will guide us through the sun and the rain.

"And we know that all things work together for good to them that love God, to them who are called according to His purpose." Romans 8:28

REFLECTION AND NOTES

The next time it rains, sit as the rain falls, close your eyes and listen to the sound of the rain and listen to what you hear or feel in that moment.

Many of us like to sit out and take in the sunshine. So the next opportunity to take in the sun's warmth let God speak to your inner being. In both instances take the time to reflect on what is happening in your life in that time and space and take inventory and notes. This should give you insight to where you currently are and where you want to go.

ROOM TO JOURNAL

_____

_____

_____

_____

_____

_____

_____

_____

_____

_____

_____

_____

_____

HOPE YOU ENJOYED
THE JOURNEY!

When we plan a trip, we become excited of the thought of all the places we plan to visit.

When you complete a trip you usually have pictures and memories for a lifetime.

I pray and hope this book sparked that in your spirit and every trip you have taken or will take will find you doing the preparation by reading God's word, incorporating prayer into your lifestyle and fostering a relationship with Him while on your trip and or journey.

Your destination will be an experience of a lifetime once you exit the car.

There are three appendixes I have included at the end of this book. They are separated into the following headlines: ACRONYMS, SITTING, and LISTENING EXERCISES. At the end of each, there is also FOOD FOR THOUGHT and PRAYERS.

The Holy Spirit has given me instructions to repeat these words. As they reenter your mind, I pray that you ponder them and think beyond what you know. My hope is that you refer to these lessons and share them with others. Whatever you do, allow them to redirect you emotionally, spiritually and physically. Use the exercises, reread the lessons, meditate on the words and let them transform your life.

APPENDIX 1

ACRONYMS

HOPE

Defined as an optimistic state of mind that is based on an expectation of positive outcomes with the respect to events and circumstances in one's life or the world at large.

Healing–When we believe for something to be healed in our life, we have an expectation of a favorable outcome. Our hope and trust should be in and focused on God.

Optimism–Being optimistic in God means we have put our confidence in Him and not in man. Knowing that all things God works together for the good of those who love God. Our future is in his Hands.

Prayer/Peace- When we allow our hope and trust to be in God, praying about everything and believing he knows what is best for us, his peace then overshadows all the fear and doubt, and we can rest in his Peace.

Everlasting/Expectation—*When we are expecting something the anticipation of it can either bring excitement or anxiety to our spirit. We all have heard this saying "we hope for the best but prepare for the worst."*

PRAYER

My HEALING, however it manifests itself I will trust God; and will be OPTIMISTIC knowing my confidence is in Him, which will give me the best outcome; with PRAYER and supplication, letting my request be known, I can rest in his PEACE while he works it out for my good; and my EXPECTATIONS are all predicated on God knowing what is best, and in the end, he promised EVERLASTING Life to those who believe in him and have put their TRUST, FAITH and HOPE in him

The question is why do we do this and find ourselves feeling hopeless? We give up, and do not believe God for the best outcome for our lives? Or we want, what we think is best?

The word says, "Faith is the substance of things hoped for, evidence of things not seen".

Whether we see anything materializing, our hope and trust still must be rooted and grounded in God's word and promises. He promised us Everlasting life if we believe in him, trusting in knows everything.

Appendix 2

Sitting And Listening Exercises

Exercise One:

Goal of this exercise is to learn who you are, spending time with yourself and God.

I would encourage everyone to do this daily

JOURNAL your day in three phases:

Morning, Afternoon, and Night, as well as indicate the Month, Date, Year and time (e.g., 00/0/00, 7:00 am). Also pray before you journal each time, and after ask God to allow the Holy Spirit to speak to you.

Why I suggest you do it this way is because you will discover patterns, behaviors and rituals that we all do or fall into. Change can be difficult, but many times there are changes God wants to make in our lives, and we need to hear from him. This helped me in the process and I stayed committed to see a fruitful outcome.

I found when I chronicled by day, I was able to go back and see things I needed to change and start praying about.

You will be amazed how when you start praying, how changes will be revealed to you through the Holy Spirit and how He will guide you and instruct you in making the necessary changes in your life.

It is a process, and if you stay committed to the process you will see the evidence in how opportunities, ideas, and prayer time will even be different.

I will tell you; this changed my life, as it has been the catalyst to my writing and spending time with God.

Tidbit: Your journal can be electronic, but if you are old school, get your pen and a Journal book and write, write, write.

EXERCISE TWO:

The Goal here is to strengthen your faith and work through situations with God's word and to develop patience.

Step One:

Sit in your quiet time and think of a situation or thing you are struggling with or believing God for a break- through in (for instance your finances, health, or marriage).

Step Two:

Go to the Word of God and identify five scriptures on the topic that speaks to your heart and pray over them. I chose five because that represents God's grace and favor.

Step Three:

Daily recite the scriptures each over your situation or circumstance until there is a breakthrough.

The breakthrough can be in many different forms depending on the situation or circumstance. Do not become discouraged if nothing is happening right away. It is in God's time; remember He is going to get the glory.

Many times, God wants to see if you will stay the course no matter what it looks like or feels like.

Just when we are ready to give up, and we think all hope is gone, that is when our healing comes, or when we lose our confidence, that is when God holds us in his arms and reminds us we belong to him.

Step Four:

Praise him before and after there is a break through. Praise him and honor him for it. Never ever forget who brought you through

Tidbit:

Keep the scriptures electronically and refer to them whenever needed. Or keep them in a notebook also put the date, time and year the breakthrough occurred. Watch God move in your life. Please take notes.

I am not going to tell you a situation or circumstance may not present itself again, but you know what to do now.

You won't have to lose any sleep over it and because you continually praise him for the break through, he will keep breaking down those walls.

He is a relational God, so you have to keep him in the mix, and you have to pray and read his word.

Don't stop. Keep going.

EXERCISE THREE:

The goal is to release those things and people from your life who present negative energy.

Step One

If you need an area of your life strengthened, such as your Faith, Love Walk, and forgiveness, etc.

Take the acronym from the Appendix, and read daily the encouraging words used to apply to each letter.

Step Two

Identify three things that are holding you back in the specific area identified and find three scriptures for you where God the Father, Jesus his son and the Holy Spirit speak to those areas (e.g., Love-difficulty expressing Love, Fear of Loving someone else, I don't know how to Love myself, I look for Love in all the wrong type of people).

and read them daily over those things and claim the victory.

Step Three

Thank God daily and write things as they begin to change as you confront the issue(s) head on with God leading and guiding you.

Tidbit:

You probably will find that you will purge numbers from your cell phone as you are freed, many people currently in your life will be released.

You will likely assess your friendships and what Value, if any to you or to the other person. This one will cause some hurt and pain as decisions will have to be made.

Let God take over; many times, he can move mountains and hills we have not even encountered yet.

EXERCISE FOUR:

Goal: Building a Stronger Relationship
Building Communication Skills
Learning How to Give and Reciprocate Love Unconditionally

Relationship Exercise
Five Love Languages
By Gary Chapman

Step One:

If you are in a relationship or contemplating entering into one I suggest you read " The Five Love Languages together as a part of Date night or time you both set aside and discuss the languages and how they relate to you both.

Step Two:

Take the Love Language Assessment to determine how you and your mate speak to the Love Languages.

Step Three:

Discuss with each other, and start incorporating the love languages that represents you both. You will find that as you acknowledge the different love languages you will respect one another's ideas and differences that attracted you to one another. Also, you will complement each other more in showing love in the languages you both possess.

Tidbit:

Always respect each other's love languages and when one is not being met discuss openly.

Never use the love languages against each other.

Yes you can have more than one of the Five Love Languages. Most will have a primary and a secondary.

My love languages are receiving gifts, and quality time.

EXERCISE FIVE:

The goal is to learn to accept who you are.

Change Those Areas You See Requiring Work

God Become the Center of Your Life to Accomplish the Goals He Has set forth for your life

Step One: Write a letter to yourself and express who you are in the letter and anything you would like to change and how you would accomplish it.

Date it and sign it and start working on the changes. Start with the MOST difficult first and work through each one.

Pray and ask God, who has he made you to be, and help you to identify that in you. If you already know this, then ask for guidance to build you up.

Step Two: After 2 months, re- write the letter and see where you have made changes.

Your re-write after several months should read like an accomplishment letter to yourself.

Step Three: Read your letters and if there is anything not accomplished it is probably something you have been afraid to tackle or not sure how to get it done.

This should become a long-term goal with specific steps to reach the goal asking God to help you, first with your Faith Walk and any obstacles.

Tidbit:

Don't shy away from the goal(s) you haven't met. Get help if necessary, and do not be afraid to ask for help.

Pray about who you should get involved to help you.

I did this and the one goal and task I found daunting was writing this book, if you are reading these exercises or the book, it has been published.

Hallelujah!

EXERCISE SIX:

Goal: Develop Non-Verbal Communication Skills

Step One: Two people, stand facing each other, and hold each other's hands.

Step Two: For five minutes look into each other's eyes, no talking. Trust me this is an exercise that will challenge you because most of us do not make eye contact or be quiet and still for even a second.

Step Three: See how long you both were able to do the Exercise, before one of you either, spoke, lost eye contact, or dropped your hands. Check the clock, and wherever you are on the clock the goal is to get to five minutes.

Step Four: Work on this until you both can do the exercise for five minutes. This will take time if you do the exercise correctly

Tidbit:

There is no right or wrong in this exercise. You will find how much your body language says or does not say to others. When you get to five minutes, push yourself to go to six minutes. Keep going, you will be amazed how you now look at your body language and others. When I did this, I realized my body language did not always reflect what I was feeling. Still not at five minutes yet. I am at two minutes. Remember this is a shared exercise, so who ever breaks first that is the time for both of you. I would suggest, as you successfully get beyond each minute, then talk about the challenges you both encountered together. This is to develop both your non-verbal communication skills and verbal communication skills.

EXERCISE SEVEN:

The goal here is to develop listening skills

Step One: Read the "LISTEN" acronym and the types of listening skills we utilize daily.

Step Two: Get a partner who can participate in this Exercise with you. Each one of you will read something to the other person.

Step Three: The person listening will close their eyes and take in what they hear. Then they will share what they heard. Discuss together.

Reverse roles and repeat.

Tidbit:

Sit together and discuss what you heard and listen to each other.

Listening skills developed to hear from God.

SITTING AND LISTENING EXERCISES

Talk less and listen more

I pray as you try any of these exercises it will give you skills to better yourself and others.

Share them with others, as I have shared them with you.

I pray that some of the exercises I have shared will help you navigate and better equipped you as you are on your journey.

These are exercises that I have done in my own life's journey and some I do periodically to see where I am presently and the growth that has occurred.

There is no methodology to these exercises; many are God inspired. Others I have learned through my training as a Certified Christian Pastoral Counselor.

APPENDIX 3

FOOD FOR THOUGHT

LOVE-

Defined as strong affection for another arising out of kinship or personal ties maternal love for a child or attraction based on sexual desire.

The biblical reference is in 1 Corinthians 13:4-8

Love is Agape—Unconditional love, love is patient, love is kind, love is not envious or boastful or arrogant or rude. It does not insist on its own way; it is not irritable or resentful; it does not rejoice in wrongdoing but rejoice in truth. Love never ends.

There are several types of LOVE:

Agape- Love is unconditional you expect nothing or desire anything. You accept it as it is presented with no conditions to receive it. Highest level of love offers.

Eros- Love of the Body (sexual desire and affection). Displayed through physical affection through touch.

Ludas—Is a childlike love commonly found in the beginning stages of a relationship (honeymoon stage).

Mania- an obsessive love towards a partner. It leads to unwanted jealously or possessiveness- known as co- dependency.

Philautia—is a healthy form of love where you recognize your- self-worth and do not ignore your personal needs. Self-love.

Philia—Love without romantic attraction and occurs between friends and family members, "brotherly love" which represents the sincere and platonic love

Storage- Love of children based on natural feelings and effortless love. A natural love of parents and children.
(Ftd.com).

Light- *Jesus is the light of the World. He is "LOVE" (John 8:12). "I am the light of the World. Whoever follows me will never walk-in darkness but will have the light of life."*

Light in this world is the love of Jesus. Light gives us the ability to see and brings illumination and truth.

Openness—*When something or someone is open, it allows them to express freely their feelings and opinions. We all have heard the expression, "Be Open to Love". What does that really mean?*

When you open your heart to the possibilities of love or receiving love, you are allowing something to come into you and release those things that need to come out.

When this happens and we release forgiveness, hate, anger etc., this frees us so true love and light can come into our heart. God is Love, OPEN you heart and let him in.

Vulnerability—*When we find ourselves vulnerable, we open ourselves or are exposed to possibly being attacked or harmed physically or emotionally. When we open ourselves to the love of God, showing our vulnerability we are saying, I love you unconditionally and I open myself up so your love and light can and will flow through you.*

Enlightenment—*When we become enlightened, there is awareness and greater knowledge and understanding about a subject. When we aspire to learn about a subject we study. Love is an emotion that we should want to have a better understanding of. How do we do this? Study God's word and read scriptures on how he showed Love with no conditions or looking for anything in return.*

When we seek Love, in all the wrong places we cheat ourselves of God's purity of Love. If God is love, we should look to him to enlighten us, in how to love and seek him

His LOVE requires us to love one another unconditionally.

TRUTH

Truth is defined as: that which is true in accordance with fact or reality.

Trust- *When we say we trust someone or something what should that mean? They speak their truth (facts) as they see it or are, they are speaking the truth, God's truth. Our trust must be in God, not man. Yes, people will tell you things that will be truthful, but always double check the facts with God. He will tell you the unadulterated truth, even when you do not want to hear it.*

Real- *The question to ask, is it real or fake. Sometimes we all have been bamboozled (fooled), made to believe something is what it is not. Real is usually something that is genuine and not fake. The saying is "he/she is the real deal". Most of us have heard this saying. Meaning they are genuine and can be trusted. We all want to believe that we have these types of people in our lives, but if we are being honest, we have found out they are not the real deal. However, God is the real deal, nothing fake about him. He will tell you the truth even if it hurts. But wouldn't you rather have a friend like Him that will keep it REAL?*

Understanding–*For many of us understanding what is true will be difficult because so many people we surround ourselves with do not tell the truth, because they do not know or understand what truth is themselves. OR even what the truth should look like or feel like. That is why we must read God's word to understand his truth and tell his truth daily, not what we think is truth.*

Transparent—*When you are transparent you allow trust to guide you as you have nothing to hide. You are honest and credible when you speak to others. You let others see who you really are. Will the real person stand up and speak God's truth, not your truth.*

God is so transparent; he wants us to see Him for who He is. He hides nothing from us. He shows us who he is every day. Are we real with Him, and show Him who we are, and seek him, so we can learn how to be transparent with him and others?

Honesty—*All the previous letters and words bring us to the bottom line. Are you an honest, truthful, real, and transparent individual or are you faking it? God already knows our flaws and what help we need. Be honest and real with Him allowing him to come into your heart so you can speak his TRUTH.*

LISTEN

Listen is defined as: gives one's attention to sound.

In my studies I learned there are four types of listening:

Appreciative, Empathic, Comprehensive, and Critical.

Appreciative is listening for enjoyment. I.e., music, motivational speaker or sermon

Empathic listening is to show mutual concern, where you concentrate on the speaker and not yourself.

Comprehensive listing is the ability to understand what you are listening to and comprehend the message that is being sent. This listening type can be difficult, as it requires you to concentrate as well as a participant in the process.

Critical listening is where you are listening to evaluate the content of the message. As a critical listener you are listening to all parts of the message, analyzing it, evaluating what was heard. When using this listening skill, you also are engaging in critical thinking. Once the information is received, you then can decide if the information is valid.
(*courses.lumenlearning.com*)

Learn- I am sure many of you have heard the term "Learn to listen." Also, "you are a great listener." Or "Would you stop talking for a minute and listen."

Or "If you had listened you wouldn't be in this mess."

Our Father, God has given us, also tools to learn how to listen to him, such as our ear, the Holy Spirit, prayer time, and his word. If we learned to listen using these tools, we would be equipped to appreciate hearing the beauty in his voice and listening to him. As we learn to listen to his voice, we would learn to be more Empathic, showing mutual concern listening more intensely to the speaker our Father. As our listening skills become more acute to hear and listen, then the critical listening skills reflect how we then can sit and evaluate what was said to us by our Father and prepare ourselves, because we now can comprehend what we heard as we concentrate on the messenger and his message to you. God is the greatest listener, because he can hear our thoughts before we even open our mouths. So, learn to use the tools we have at our fingertips to LISTEN to him.

Inner- We all have an Inner voice that gives us the ability to hear and listen. We can hear things constantly in our inner spirit, but the question is will you go beyond this and Listen. Allowing our ear to only accept the inner voice of God, through his holy spirit living inside. No matter, where you are in your relationship with God, he is waiting for you to come to him so he can start speaking to you. The Inner peace will have you listening to his every word.

Sound/Spirit- What a sound when we have a listening ear for hearing from God. His voice and sound will drown out all other rhetoric. His sound is music to your ear. Your spirit will also have a new sound where it will rejoice when you hear his voice. He will leap for joy, because "my child you not only heard me you listened and acted on what you heard".

Talk- Although, talking is essential to communicating our thoughts and feelings to others, there has to be a time to stop "talking" and listen for a response to what was said. Prayer is like that, where we have a conversation with God our Father through prayer and worship time with him. Then comes the point where we need to listen to the response. Knowing you can have this time becomes a resting time to reflect and open both your heart and ear to let him talk to you while you listen.

Ear- Hearing is the key to listening. We can hear physically or Spiritually. If for some reason one has limitations in hearing *physically, if we spend time with him, God's voice can be heard with the inner voice through his Holy Spirit. Our ear brings the sound of his voice into our spirit.*

Notes- *When we take notes, we have heard something and listened, and now we put it on paper to recall or retain for later. When we listen to our Father, we should take notes so we will be clear as to what we heard while listening to his voice. The Bible is the greatest notebook, many of the stories were written by inspiration of someone hearing from God and listening and putting it to the memory on paper. We should practice this in our time spent in hearing and listening to God. Take notes, read them and allow them to speak to you, listen to the inner voice of the Holy Spirit and take action.*

PEACE

Peace is defined as: a state of tranquility or quiet. The bible speaks to spiritual peace as a state of having inner peace mentally and Spiritually. Having knowledge and understanding to keep oneself strong in the face of discord or stress.

Inner peace from God comes when we pray and meditate quietly, spending time with him daily. In this time God's Holy Spirit will give you peace and comfort you. His spirit is a Comforter and will give you peace.

John 14: 16-17

"And I will pray the Father, and he shall give you another comforter, that he may abide with you forever.

Prayer—*Prayer is the key to all things and the gateway to God's truth through the Holy Spirit that brings peace and comfort. Prayer brings us into a relationship with God daily where our inner peace is tapped into allowing him to enter and reside in us. Prayer biblically in Hebrew is to interact with God to give thanks or changing a situation. Remember we cannot change anything or anyone. Only God can do that.*

Easiness—*When you feel ease you are free from worry and discomfort. Praying and meditating on God's word brings this state of being as you allow the Holy Spirit to dictate your movement through life comforting you with PEACE. Do not look at the situation, look at God.*

Amen—*When we hear the word Amen, what does it represent? Usually when praying at the end of the prayer you may hear Amen. It means, "so be it". It is finished; done nothing else needs to be said. When we pray and the holy spirit Speaks, "God has spoken", so all one has to do is say AMEN and let the Peace of God abide as you trust, believing that all things are in his hands as his WILL is done.*

Calm- *The PEACE of God has a calming influence over us when we pray and trust him to do what is best for us, no matter the circumstances or situation we may find ourselves in.*

Endurance–*When we endure, it usually means we have come through a difficult or challenging time in our life. We all, at some point has or will face these times. The word of God speaks to how we should endure in him. "Be anxious for nothing but in everything by prayer and supplication with Thanksgiving let your request be known unto God". Philippians 4:6. This Scripture many quotes, now is the time to really trust God live it out as we endure the many challenges of life today.*

PRAYER

Peace can only come from God, no man, woman, or child can give the PEACE He can. It brings EASINESS in storms that only he can give and in PRAYER time at the end you thank him and say AMEN. Then a CALM breeze will overtake you where you will be able to ENDURE anything with God resting in his PEACE.

REVELATION

Defined as: a surprising and previously unknown fact or a divine supernatural disclosure to humans.

Retina (eye) Reveal
External- *see outward what has been seen inward*
Vision- *to see through the eyes of Jehovah*
Eyes–*open the eyes of my heart*
Almighty God, let me see you
Love- *there is love and life in God's reveal.*
Alert- *be prepared to receive the revelation*
Time- *there is timing in God's revelation.*

Insight- brings ability to see beyond your eye, spiritual eye
Open- open my eyes that I may see you Jehovah
Night Vision—your light shines by the moonlight, so we are able
to see even at night.

PRAYER

When we have REVELATION from God it says we are in a rela-
tionship and we communicate daily in Prayer and Worship. Which
then opens our eyes and ears where secrets are REVEALED
EXTERNALLY with the vision of God where then our EYES
are open to the ALMIGHTY and being ALERT daily to hear
from him. The LOVE of God never lets you be blind-sided, and
TIMING will reveal all things. Through INSIGHT of seeing
beyond the naked eye (spiritually) then we can open ourselves to
receive the vision even in the darkness of NIGHT. God gives light
by the moon to even reveal himself. He leaves no stone unturned
in his REVELATION.

GRIEF

Defined as: Mental suffering or distress over affliction, or loss of
someone. Painful regret causing distress and sorrow

Five and Seven stages of Grief:

The five stages of grief are: Denial, Anger, Bargaining, Depression,
and Acceptance

The seven stages of grief are:

Shock and Denial, Pain and Guilt, Anger and Bargaining, Depression, The Upward Turn, Reconstruction and Working through, Acceptance and Hope

Not everyone will experience every stage of Grief. Whichever one you experience there is no specific timeframe in the healing process. Everyone will be different, so do not compare yourself to anyone else in their handling of the Grief process.

GRIEF

The Holy Spirit gave this Acronym to work through Grief in a different way with God

God–*allow God to be the Center of your Heart, and spirit not the Guilt. Let him massage your heart with his love replacing the loss and the feelings associated with it. I am not saying you will not have feelings of loss but let God sooth you. It will come in time but stay in love with him and he will give you Peace.*

Reflection / Restoration–*when we have loss in our lives, we usually lose our joy and purpose to our lives. This is the time we should draw our strength and reflect on the good times had and things associated with the things we now will gain not what was loss. Many times, when we lose something or someone, we feel emptiness or, a void in our heart. God is the only one that can restore what we have loss. No, he cannot bring our love ones back, but he can bring and put people in our lives that can help us get back on track in the healing process.*

Inspiration—this is the time to be inspired by the word of God. Read scriptures that will sooth your heart, spirit, and encourages you. Never give up in the midst of a storm.

Energize—yourself with prayer, meditating on his word and then allowing him to revive your spirit and joy in him.

Fight vs. Flight- this is the time we should stand still and see the Salvation of God. Let him fight the battle for you. Usually your strength will be limited, and you will have no fight in you. Do not take flight either, running away does not allow for the healing of your loss. Running away is only a short-term solution. God is the only solution.

I know many will say some will need professional help to deal with their loss.

I agree if the circumstances warrant it, seek help. Even pray about whom you should seek professional help from. God knows exactly what you will need.

Scriptures on grief to help you navigate the process

TELEVISION

Television is defined as: a system of transmitting visual images and sound that are reproduced on screens, used to broadcast programs for entertainment, information and education

God is telling "His" "story" (History). Have you turned on the Tell a Vision (Television)? Are you on the right Channel? The stories are endless. The Bible is a book of his story and how we are to live out our lives. The metaphor is the TV and are we watching and seeing the story unfold for our lives as God sees it.

Tell *a story, when you tell a story visually it brings to life something someone has imagined and is able to bring it out for others to see. Thus, tell and show the vision.*

Eyes—*Our eyes are the gate way to sight, which gives us the ability to see. The eye can focus on the visual story telling.*

Light- *As light beams into our eye our sight is crisp and illuminates the story with vivid color which allows our imagination to flow as the story unfolds.*

Eyesight—*Physical ability to see in the natural state. What are you allowing yourself to see?*

Visual/Vivid- *when we see something visually it is the ability to have sight, a picture, or display to illustrate something. The vividness of the site addresses the clarity and crispness of what you see through your sight.*

Insight- *inwardly what do you see beyond you telling and showing visual story to others. What is God showing you in your story?*

Sight/Sound–*Oh, what do I see when my eyes are open and focused on God in my story and is the sound of his voice in my ear to hear.*

Illuminate–*Your story visually should bring out the inner spirit and the light of God should shine through your story*

Optical (*clarity*)–*Physical light brings sight but we must do some soul searching for the spiritual light of God.*

News- *When you are watching television it is the news, giving you a rundown of the day's events. Our good news is the Gospel of Jesus Christ and the many Miracles and signs he has shown and given us. Truly newsworthy.*

When the tell a vision and story is told through the visual medium of TV, and the Director, God says, lights, camera and action what will your story reveal. Will it be the story you wanted to be shown or the true story that God wanted to reveal? Let God tell and show your story through his eyes and radiant light with vivid color and clarity.

BIBLE *is defined as*
Book of
Information
Brought to
Life to live by while on the
Earth

The BIBLE has 66 books of stories that we can reference and is relevant to present day life. If you take some time and read it you will find a story that speaks to your life, and all of what is going on in the World today, and what will go on until the end of this World and God returns.

Pick it up, it is easier now than ever with the technological advances. Your fingertips on a computer, laptop, Smartphone or IPAD and you are tapped into the Book of Information Brought to Life to live by while on the Earth- BIBLE.

PAIN AND HURT

Prayer *will start the healing process from which the pain originates. Knowing the root cause of the pain and hurt. It can be physical or spiritual.*

Answers *come when knowing the root or origin of the pain. The opening of yourself to acknowledge the pain and in prayer, God will unfold and reveal answers and solutions will emerge.*

Internally *when we pray and listen for answers our heart and mind will be open and be able to receive or accept the answers allowing the healing process to begin.*

Newness—*A new person will emerge out of the Ashes of Pain, with prayer, answers, internally having God working on them and the NEW person emerges out of a place of PAIN.*

Heart of the Matter. *When your heart has been broken, usually we have been misled; abused, mistreated the list can go on and on. When do we put on the brakes and allow healing to come into the mix.*

Understanding *is the key to knowing why we are hurting and what caused the pain and hurt? The word again is forgiveness. Everything starts and ends with this word if you want to conquer Pain and Hurt.*

LEARNING FORGIVENESS.

Rejuvenation *will come once you are able to master the first two letters of the word HURT. You will become whole in your heart, spirit, soul, mind and body.*

Time, *they say heals all wounds. Although we cannot truly measure time, as we live it moves and as it moves so will the healing process move forward through time. Each day the Hurt and Pain will ease as you walk in total forgiveness.*

There is no getting around it, Oh, and you must forget.

(If you read the book). I do not have to say another word (LOL).

PRAYER

PAIN and HURT go hand in hand, usually when we are in pain we hurt and when we hurt, we are in pain, whether it is physical, spiritual or emotional.

When we are in this state, PRAYER is the key to starting the healing process. Prayer will open the door to a relationship with God, as he will give you ANSWERS as to how to deal with the pain and hurt, bringing you INTERNALLY a peace in your mind, body and soul as you allow him to rest in you and make you a NEW person.

As we embody the new person, we must allow the Hurt associated with the pain to be washed away. Allowing our HEART to be washed and cleansed by God showing us how to forgive ourselves, and others. Then having the UNDERSTANDING where the Hurt and Pain originated from and the courage to acknowledge it and forgive. This will rejuvenate your spirit, where God can become the Center of our Joy daily, and over TIME you will look in the rear-view mirror and drive as fast as the speed limit will allow, never to look at the Hurt and Pain that kept you in bondage ever again.

WISDOM

The word Wisdom can be interpreted in many ways. I am going to speak to the biblical and Godly definition of the word. Godly Wisdom In the biblical context, it characterized as having a deep understanding, keen Discernment and a capacity for sound judgment, being wise

Wise—When one is wise, you have insight and understanding above and beyond what you could imagine or see. This is a gift from God. Yes, we can be wise in other things, but when God is the barrier of wisdom, the levels exceed our understanding or abilities.

Intelligence—When God gave me this word and looked it up it gave me a different prospective on the usage of the word. It describes "Intel" as useful information concerning a subject of interest (such as an enemy). Intelligence fresh and accurate resulting in a successful operation. I now see the connection in being wise and having Godly Wisdom.

This gives you an upper hand to your enemies, where you are given special information that would allow you to overtake those who would try to hurt or harm you. The holy spirit, giving special instructions or how to handle the situation with Godly wisdom

Spirit—When the Godly Wisdom is activated your spirit is in tune to the ear of God, and you can follow the instructions specifically to what and how you are to go. The Holy Spirit will lead, guide, instruct, bring comfort and peace beyond all understanding.

Discernment—When God has given us this gift, it allows him to give spiritual guidance and understanding. You have the perception as well as the ability to judge well. In the biblical context, you can determine God's desire in a situation or for one's life. Being able to identify the true nature of things such as good and evil. If you have been blessed with this gift, use it Wisely.

Openness—When something has been opened, it allows something to go in or come out. Godly wisdom is like this, it flows in and out. The door will open allowing the Wisdom of God to flow through you, and when there is something that presents evil, the door will close to protect you or give insight to protect others.

Mercy- Mercy is such a wonderful gift from God. Even when we mess up and do not follow Godly Wisdom, he gives us New Mercy daily to repent and start fresh.

PRAYER

Prayer is defined as: a solemn request for HELP or expression of thanks addressed to God or object if Worship.

Peace- when we allow the flow of peace to abide in our spirit we then can open our hearts and pray allowing God's Holy Spirit to comfort us.

Revelation—when we speak to God in prayer and his spirit speaks to us he will reveal secrets and mysteries as only he can do.

Advocate- God is the greatest Advocate that we can have. He gave us the Holy Spirit to lead and guide us to all truth. Prayer time is the best time.

Yielding- *when we yield to the Holy Spirit in prayer time and listen to God the possibilities are endless of what he will share with you.*

Evolution—when we evolve we are changing into who he would have us to be which allows God to use us for his glory.

Righteousness—when we allow God to live in us we will be in right standing living a Holy life, where his holy spirit reigns over everything we do.

Prayer is a lifestyle that we all should aspire to. It does not happen overnight but over time spent with God daily. The Peace will show in spending prayer time, he will reveal things in your quite prayer time. He will comfort you in prayer time as he is the greatest Advocate (Holy Spirit) to defend you. And as we yield to the Holy Spirit, we will evolve (a changed person) into a righteous and holy human being living a lifestyle of Godliness.

HEALING

Healing is defined as: a process of restoration of health from an unbalance diseased, damaged, or vitalized organism. In the biblical sense, it is a divine intervention as in a response prayer and faith

Healthy- *something that God revealed as I was praying in this word Healthy as two words 'heal" "thy". What jumped out at me was when we are healthy in both spirit, body, mind and soul (spirit) we are healthy, and Thy will (God's) is being done when we are walking in total healing*

Eternal–*peace and forgiveness is the key to your healing lasting or existing forever. Once God has healed you from a situation and or circumstance, wholeness in your physical and spiritual body is a constant for eternity.*

Authority–*in the healing process we must relinquish authority to God physically and Spiritually so he can work on us in his "operating room" surgically putting the pieces physically back together to function properly as well as our heart spiritually of the brokenness so we can be HEALED.*

Love- *our HEARTS are the gateway to LOVE and once we allow God to be the healer and complete the open HEART surgery the Chambers of the heart and blood flow will pump normally revitalizing the body Physically and Spiritually.*

Intervention–*many times we have required someone to intervene in our lives to help us or to redirect us on a new pathway. When God causes an INTERVENTION, it is to correct or redirect us. HEALING is exactly what occurs when we allow him to step in and correct those things that prevent us from being HEALED and DELIVERED and set free.*

Newness–*healing brings newness in our spirit and being. Physically and spiritually our body is revitalized with energy and strength to do the work and walk in our purpose and destiny and plan of God for our lives.*

Goodness–*God's GOODNESS in the healing process brings MERCY to the table of HEALING. He already knows what* *we will need to be victorious in our healing, so he is patient with us, holding our hand through the process assuring us HE is with us. We must believe in him and trust, that the outcome will be the best in the HEALING process.*

Remember Healing is a process that you must go through with God's HELP and direction. Again, FORGIVENESS is the ultimate key to your total healing.

APPENDIX 4

"Fire"

MARVELOUS LIGHT

All the parts of our physical body must work together for the fire of God's power to burn, ignite and build us up in the fire of the Holy Spirit.

First let us look at the acronym for fire:

F-FIRE is defined as the combustion or burning where substances combine chemically with Oxygen from the air and typically give off a bright, light, mixed with heat, and smoke or a burning sensation in the body. It also can be defined as a *flame*. A hot glowing body of ignited gas that is generated by something on fire is sometimes referred to as a *flame*. Trees can catch on *fire* without assistance with the wind shifting in the presence of the tiniest spark.

I- IGNITE cause to catch on fire without any assistance or set on fire with assistance. Keep this in mind the next time you light a gas stove or a bar-b-queue grill. Consider yourself as assisting in making a *fire*. Be responsible whenever you *ignite*.

R- RESTORE to bring back to previous state, return to former condition, place, or position, repair, refurbish, rebuild, refine, reconstruct, remodel, makeover. What is it that you want God's *fire* to do?

E-ENGULFED to surrounded or be covered up completely. Make sure your heart does not send you down the wrong path in your journey because it is *engulfed* in anything negative.

Second let us look at some biblical correlations to God's *fire*.

We know that God /Jehovah made us in His image and likeness. We are the only physical living creatures He did this with.

In Genesis 1:26-28, we see that God made man and woman after His own image and likeness.

In Exodus 24:17, fire represents God's radiant glory or holiness and can be used as a metaphor that represents purification.

In Exodus 33:18, Moses asked God to please show him His glory. The appearance of the Glory of the Lord was like a devouring fire on the top of the mountain in the sight of the people of Israel.

In Exodus 13:21, we are told that the Lord guided the Israelites out of bondage and into freedom led in a pillar of cloud by day and a pillar of fire by night.

Ask yourself what dark places or night situations you want the light of God's fire to illuminate.

Finally, in Hebrew 12:29, our hearts are warmed and illuminated by God's consuming fire. When you consume something, you overtake it or overpower it.

Fire is referenced in God's Word 627 times–524 Old Testament and 103 times in the New Testament. The words associated with fire in the word of God are:

1) *Flame* is referenced 74 times;

2) *Blaze* is referenced 27 times:

3) *Burn* is referenced 245 times;

4) To *Ignite* is referenced 11 times;

5) To *Kindle* is referenced 27 times:

6) *Smoke* is referenced 127 times;

7) *Ashes* is referenced 53 times.

Other mentions you might want to read and consider in these mentions are:

A) Matthew 6:22

B) Luke 3:16

C) Genesis 2:7

D) Psalm 18:8

E) Job 41: 20-21

F) Proverbs 18:21

G) Habakkuk 3:4

H) Deuteronomy 4:12-13

I) I Rev 1:15

J) Rev 2:18

K) Matt 5:8

L) Psalm 51

M) Proverbs 23:26

N) Matt 22:27

O) Psalm 10:3

P) Luke 11:33-36

Let us look at the principles surrounding the descent of the Holy Spirit upon the apostles that brought fire to their ears and made their mouths speak in different tongues. How do we accomplish and keep the fire and light in our eye? We must cover the four principles, Holy Spirit, praying, fasting, His Word.

In chapter 2 of the Acts of the Apostles, from verses 2 thru 28, we see the descent of the Holy Spirit which is the promise and gift Jehovah, or God, or Yahweh that was left for us to (lead us, guide us, instruct us, bring us comfort, and bring us peace, to help us). Apostle Denise C. Davis

THE FIRST PRINCIPAL IS THE HOLY SPIRIT AS OUR ADVOCATE

In Matthew 6:5, we are taught how to pray, and it includes how the Holy Spirit can instruct us through the fire.

The Lord's Prayer is the blueprint to follow as we go through the fire and enter the throne room of grace to worship Him in spirit and in truth.

THE SECOND PRINCIPAL IS PRAYER

Matthew 6:16 instructs us to fast quietly and only in the eyes of God to keep our bodies clean. Fasting quietly and not for show is important as we continue through the fire.

THE THIRD PRINCIPAL IS FASTING QUIETLY TO CLEAN THE BODY

In Psalm 119: 105, 130, it explains that since our words can be mightier than the sword, so to speak, they should always be chosen carefully so that they can continue to be the lamp that lights the fire under our feet. When our pathway has constant light unfolding for our pathway, the journey is much simpler.

THE FOURTH PRINCIPAL IS TO MAKE SURE OUR WORDS ARE CAREFULLY

CHOSEN SO THEY ARE ALWAYS A LIGHT UNDER OUR FEET.

To close out these principles let us say we want to be rooted and grounded in the fire.

We can see that when we pray for the Holy Spirit to guide us, God will reveal to us what we need to do on our journey.

When we can smell God's fire in our nostrils, from the smoke of His fire, can feel God's fire burning inside of us when we pray, our physical senses will ignite our spiritual flame.

ANALOGY

As our physical being and our senses work and operate in the fire of His radiant, illuminating fire in the Holy Spirit our five senses come into play.

The five senses of the physical body all can see, smell what is burning, feel the warmth of the fire, be burned when we touch the fire, taste and/or hear fire.

Each part of the body is important to the functioning of our physical being. Although, this may be true our spiritual being is what will sustain us in the fire of the Holy Spirit.

Therefore, if your body is full of light as when a lamp shines its light on you, keep in mind the fire of God's light will be reflected in and through our eyes, nostrils, mouth/tongue, hands, ears and feet.

God gave us five senses—the ability to see, smell, taste, touch, and hear. Each one of these senses is associated with one of our body parts that become the portal to release and receive God's fire in the Holy Spirit.

So let us explore the eye, nostrils, mouth/tongue, and the hand in God's fire.

1. Fire in your eyes- "The eye is the lamp of the body. If your eyes are healthy your whole body will be full of light it allows us to see/ sight/ insight

In the fire you have the ability physically/Spiritually to see God's glory/fire to discern" (Matt. 6:22).

Wisdom which gives spiritual insight

Physically it gives ability to see/perception (fire, flames and smoke)

Spiritually the eye is symbolic of light to the entire body allowing us to see in the spiritual realm of the fire of the Holy Spirit. Fire is ignited through our eyes brings (light, clarity, vision, and revelation.

If you close your eyes you will see nothing physically it becomes dark, when our eyes are open light reflects and we can focus and see our surroundings.

Now if we have the light of God's Fire in the Holy Spirit when our eyes are closed physically where no visual light can enter then the fire of His light takes over inside where His eternal flame consumes us in the spirit, and we can see beyond the naked eye.

Have you ever thought about someone who is blind and cannot see, how do they see the world, how do they process seeing?

One of their senses physically is not available. However, the fire of God can illuminate anything not visible through the portal of the physical eye.

Also, when one of the five senses physically is not functioning, other senses are heightened in the fire physically.

God will never leave us blind to His fire.

If you ever watch a blind person in the physical realm move about, they use their other senses to compensate for the lack of the other sense.

2. Fire in your nostrils- "Then the Lord God formed man from the dust of the ground and breathed the breath of life into His nostrils. Jehovah blew

His breath of fire- life into Adam" (Gen. 2:7).

"Smoke went up out of His nostrils and fire from His mouth devoured: coals were kindled by it" (Ps. 18:8)

– "*Out of His nostrils smoke goes forth, as from a boiling pot and burning reeds. Its breath sets coals a blaze and flames dart from His mouth.*

Nostrils allow us to breath in oxygen, which is important to our existence to live: (Job 41: 20-21.

When we smell smoke the nostrils through breathing tells us fire in around us. Sense of smell also allows us to prepare for what the fire can bring.

Awareness that the fire is imminent.

Smell also can bring a sweet odor or a stinking odor. What is in your life that smells good that we want to continue to throw logs into the fire so the smell will reinstate the sweetness of God's fire to all that when you present yourself anywhere you go or are they can smell the sweet aroma of God's presence.

Or do you have a stink smell odor that needs to be burned out in the fire.

Remember fire purifies, so when you come out of the fire there will be no stench that you had been in the fire but the aroma of God's fire will be sweet.

3.Fire in your mouth/tongue

"*Life and Death is in the power of the tongue: and they that love it shall eat the fruit thereof*" (Prov. 18:21)

The fire of God on your tongue can give life and light or bring death. What are you choosing to speak, life over death? When we speak life in the fire it can burn out what needs to be removed and build up what needs to be strengthened in the power of Jehovah.

The word of God is fire, with a flame that will never go out.

Taste the word /acquire the taste of the fire by studying His word, living His word and sharing the word.

Once you acquire a taste you will always want to eat the word because it is sweet to the tongue, you will have a fire to speak and live the word in the fire.

5. Fire in your hands/ healing power.

Hand of God- Five-Fold Ministries

Apostle- Messenger—Fire in the word

Prophet- Fire in the revelation of God

Evangelist—Fire of spreading God's word and bringing those into the fire of God

Preacher- Fire of continuing to encourage the sheep

Teacher- Fire in studying and teaching God's Word.

Apostle Denise C. Davis

"His radiance is like the sunlight, He has rays flashing from His hands, and therein is hiding of His power. Fire in the hand of God and His Ministries" (Hab. 3:4).

Just one touch from the healing hand of the fire of Jehovah Raphe will heal the sick and raise the dead. Cast out demons.

REFERENCES IN THE WORD

Woman with the issue of blood (Just one touch) she was made whole in the fire of healing Restoration to her body in the fire.

The hand of God can snatch us out of any situation/circumstances.

Hand of God is over our lives, in the fire of prayer as we worship Him daily. When we raise our hands in worship His Glory, radiates with His light/ fire illuminates and comes down and engulfs us with His glory and consuming fire/light and heat.

So God in His infinite wisdom created us and gave us specific body functions to release His fire through our five senses attached to our physical being/existence.

5. Fire in your ears—"Then the Lord spoke to you out of the fire. You heard words but saw no form; there was only a voice. He declared to you His covenant, The Ten Commandments, which He commanded you to follow and then He wrote them on two stone tablets" (Deut. 4:12-13).

Listening ear in the fire. Have you allowed your ears to be tuned into the frequency of God's Holy Spirit fire to hear the instructions of God?

What Commandments have God directed to you/your assignment(s).

When our ears have consumed the fire, it will burn out the rhetoric we hear, and give us the spiritual ability to listen to the calmness of God's fire burning in our ear.

The ability to discern the wisdom to know when you are hearing from God almighty in the fire. Keep your listening ear aligned in the spirit.

Do not let the naysayers distract you from hearing what thus says the Lord in the fire.

6. Fire in your feet– "His feet were like blazing fire and His voice was like the sound of rushing water" (Rev. 1:15).

"These are the words of the son of God, whose eyes are like blazing fire and -whose feet are like burnished bronze" (Rev. 2:1:18).

He has given us the ability to have feet of fire that can step on serpents and burn them out.

Feet that can walk out of any circumstance with the fire under our feet.

Feet that allow us to stand in the fire, they bring balance to the rest of our body.

Your physical body was designed you were wonderfully made in your mother's wound knitted together.

Spiritually when our feet have been in the fire of His light, we should come out of the fire walking with a pep in our step

Allowing the fire if the Holy Spirit to order our steps

God in His wisdom

then placed into this body a heart and soul.

So it is important that we speak about the spiritual aspect of our being/existence.

Note: physically, God gave us two of everything regarding our five senses which brings

BALANCE

However, when we speak of the fire spiritually, we have one heart and one soul inward oneness with God's fire through the Holy Spirit.

B. Spiritual connection to the body

1. Fire in your heart

Scripture: "Blessed are the pure in heart for they shall see God" (Matt. 5:8

Fire of purification comes when we allow God's will to be done in the fire. Purifying us in the fire which opens our heart to be loving, compassionate, kind, unselfish, caring about one another and being obedient.

"Create in me a clean heart and renew the right spirit within me) (Ps. 51).

"My son give me your heart and let your eyes delight in me" (Prov. 23:26).

Four principles

Heart of Fire for God

1. Converted /Saved

Accept Jesus as your Lord and savior

Invite the fire of Jesus into your heart, to live and breathe on the inside of you

2. Fire of the Holy Spirit dwell inside of you

3. Spend more time in the fire of prayer, word and worship

4. Obedient in the fire

These four principles then opens the heart to have His fire and a heart of pure love for God and others-Agape love/unconditional love

Aren't you glad God /Jehovah loves us unconditionally in all our mess He looked beyond that and sees our needs.

2. Fire in your soul

Definition of soul refers to a living breathing conscious body rather than to an immortal

soul-living being that can reason, one's character, feelings, consciousness, memory, perception, and thinking.

"Jesus replied, 'love the Lord your God with all your heart and with all your soul and with all your mind'" (Matt. 22:37.

Praise the Lord, my soul all my inmost being, praise His holy name

Your soul "How you Living" "Who are you"

Your soul is where your inner most thoughts arise "inner man" it resides in the physical body/flesh.

It speaks to how you process things, reasoning skills, characteristics/ character, perception- how you see things, cognitive ability to understand, ability to reason

The soul and mind speak and work together. Psalm 103

Definition of the "mind"

Element in an individual that feels, perceives, thinks, wills things and can reason.

SIT AND LISTENING TIME:

Our Spirit is the Connection we have to our Creator. The Holy SPIRIT FIRE dwells within us, as we foster a relationship with GOD our Father.

REFLECTION AND NOTES

God has given us all abilities in the physical realm with our bodily limbs. To see, hear, smell, touch, and to taste. Spiritually he has given us a heart and soul where his holy spirit dwells and speaks to our heart.

Are you allowing GOD to use you physically and spiritually for his Glory?

Whatever he has given you, use it and do not every take it for granted.

Yes, some will have limitations, but GOD still will use you to encourage someone else that may have the same challenge.

We all are precious in his sight, and never let your fire go out keep feeding it with his word.

FINAL THOUGHTS

As I reflected while on this journey called life, oh so many twists and turns and out of it came this book. I dragged my feet for several years before committing to write this book. I would receive revelation from God, write it down and then put it in my file drawer. This went on even when prophetic word came forth that I would write a book. As time went on, I realized I was more concerned with what people were going to think about the book than what God wanted me to do. I went into a dry spell and I was hearing nothing. I decided I would take what I had written and file it until God started giving me words to write. In July 2019, I sent what I had to the person, and it was typed up, but once I received it back mid-September and read it, I knew it needed work.

I was despondent and felt like I would have to go back to the drawing board. Everything is in God's timing, I missed the first opportunity, but He already knew I needed to experience and spend more time with Him, so he would speak through me in his time. When I allowed myself to have quiet time with him and surrendered fully my life to Him the book flowed like a river. I was writing so fast, I could hardly keep up, but he was right there with me. The summer of 2020, he took me on this journey you are now reading about. When God moves and needs you to do something, you had better have on your roller skates. As a nation, dealt with a COVID-19 pandemic, inequities, racial Injustice and so much more. I, myself, went through two hip replacements in three months and physical therapy three times a week for nearly six months.

(SHOUT OUT to Dr. Gregg Klein–Rothman Orthopedics and Dr. Martin Malaluan, PT, DPT, OCS of Teaneck Orthopedic Physical Therapy.

During that time, I spent time with God like never before`. I took up my cross and made a conscious decision to follow Him for real. "Ain't nothing like the REAL thing, baby."

REFERENCES

Jenna Birch, "7 Distinct Greek Words Describe Different kinds of Love- which have you experienced," 2019, https://www.wellandgood.com

FTD Fresh," The 8 Different types of Love and Perfect Combo for you," January 16, 2020, https://www.Ftd.com>blog>give

"Lumen- Fundamentals of Public Speaking"- Module2- Audience Analysis and Effective Listening, 2021, https://www.courses.lumenlearning.com